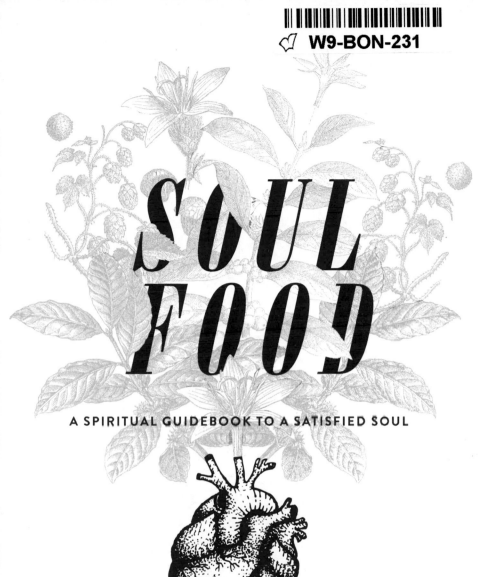

SOUL FOOD

A SPIRITUAL GUIDEBOOK TO A SATISFIED SOUL

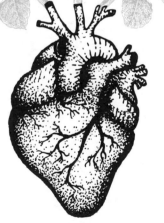

 HAVILAH CUNNINGTON

HAVILAH CUNNINGTON

I always knew God had a plan for others' lives, but never felt God could use me. I struggled with learning disabilities throughout my school years, which caused me to have great insecurity about my value and worth. It wasn't until the age of 17, as I was sitting in a car with friends on my way to a party, when I heard the voice of God speak to my heart, "There is more to life than this! I have called you. Come follow me." I spoke out in that moment, telling those in the car that I had a call on my life and they were welcome to come with me, but I was going to serve God.

I remember walking into our house when I got home, kneeling by my bed and saying these simple words, "God, I'm not much. I'm young, I'm a girl with no special gifting. But if You can use anyone, You can use me." Now, thinking back to that day, it makes me laugh how I'd hoped the heavens would have opened up, with angels descending and ascending on a heavenly ladder – that didn't happen and I didn't need it to. God heard my cry and He was at work to accomplish His perfect will in my life.

By 19, my twin sister Deborah and I were traveling all over California preaching, teaching and singing at any place that would have us. By 21, we had been in seven different states and Mexico teaching about Jesus and His great plan for this generation!

Now two decades later I still believe today is the Church's finest hour, if we choose to live with passion, purpose and walk in power. I'm passionate about seeing individuals encounter God in a real way and seek to blow the lid off common misconceptions, personal limitations and powerless living. My heart and passion is to inspire and challenge others to become all God has designed them to be.

Havilah Cunnington is a speaker, author, wife, and mother to four boys. She prayed a simple but passionate prayer as a young woman saying, "God if You can use anyone, You're welcome to use me." She is now a speaker and author of several bible studies including Radical Growth, I Do Hard Things, The Good Stuff, and Eat. Pray. Hustle. She loves the Word and consistently looks for ways to make it accessible to all, no matter their background or busy schedule. With over twenty years of full-time ministry experience, she believes today is the Church's finest hour if we choose to live with passion and purpose, walking in power. Like any true Italian, Havilah loves filling a table with good food and close friends, but her greatest Joy Is spending time with her husband, Ben, and their four young sons: Judah, Hudson, Grayson, and Beckham.

Havilah

INTRODUCTION

You are holding a devotional I couldn't wait to get into your hands.

If you follow my life or the life of Truth to Table, you will quickly learn about our yearly studies. Last year we took over 15,000 of you from over 100 nations through our New Year course.

But let me say, I didn't start out planning for all of you. I was a busy woman, like most. I was a wife and a Mom which made my daily life full and lively. Add in a ministry, a full travel schedule, meaningful relationships, and you'll begin to see how I was always looking for hours in my day.

Honestly, there wasn't a day that went by where I didn't love God or want His voice active in my everyday life. I desperately wanted to stay inspired. I wanted to lead a life surrounded by the truth that echoed my Biblical core beliefs and family values. To live authentically is one of my greatest values and, with every conversation we had, I heard you saying the same things.

I sort of stumbled onto an idea to help women (and some men too) get their daily Bible vitamin. It was a brief and fleeting thought I had one morning. I had just finished writing my second devotional, Radical Growth, and decided I wanted to walk people through it online. I didn't have any fancy cameras or staff to help me. Just me, in my kitchen, with an iPhone. I quickly posted my idea on Facebook, created an event and shared. I was hopeful someone would join me, after all, I had a Mom and a few friends. (wink) I was shocked to find that in a few short weeks over 6,000 of you and your friends joined in for our first study. What an incredible response! If we had known what was about to happen, we might have chickened out, but God is so faithful, and the growth only pushed us to create more studies to assist you in your everyday, modern lifestyle.

We are now approaching our fifth study. We've been busy dreaming and scheming, praying and obeying, for about a year, asking God what He wanted us to share with you.

As I pondered our study, I felt God highlight to me four meals in the Bible. I began to consider the meals and saw their link to the different soul 'hungers' we each have. Welcome to Soul Food! As a result of God showing me this truth, we will spend four weeks looking at the four meals of the Bible. We will identify the particular soul hunger they expose in each of us. We will examine the consequences of not nourishing these needs and God's provision and specific invitation we each receive to eat each meal.

The first meal is the apple, consumed by Adam & Eve. We look at the separation this meal creates and how it shows our hunger to be loved.

The second meal is the bread and wine offered by Jesus. We consider how the Father planned the most lavish, costly, redemptive meal ever prepared. A meal perfectly equipped to redeem the separation caused by the first meal, restoring our hunger to belong.

The third meal is the meal of milk and honey. This is the description God gave of the Promised Land, and as the Israelites moved towards the land, they were becoming the people of God. In this meal, we look at our hunger to become.

Lastly, we look at the meal of the fish and loaves; the multiplication of Jesus and His feeding of others, which reveals our appetite to partner with a miracle working God. This acknowledges our hunger to bless.

For the next 20 days, we will feast on the certainty of God's Word. Our everyday life will be nourished as we chew on truth. We will listen to our hunger pains and learn to feed our deepest hearts. Feast at the right tables. Sit with our true companion. Enjoy the soul food prepared by the Creator of the universe. This study is designed for a 20-day journey, but it also can be used as a moment-to-moment devotional. Each day holds a complete thought. You won't slide behind or feel lost if you open these pages sporadically. We've created the days to hold about eight minutes of study, with an additional five if you're feeling inspired.

So, my friend, let's jump in. I'm so happy you're here with me.
Grab your Bible, notebook and a cup of something warm and let's begin.

Pull Up A Chair

HAVILAH

APPLES +TREES

HUNGER TO BE LOVED

A deep sense of love and belonging is an irreducible need of all people. We are biologically, cognitively, physically, and spiritually wired to love, to be loved, and to belong. When those needs are not met, we don't function as we were meant to. We break. We fall apart. We numb. We ache. We hurt others. We get sick.

BRENE BROWN

The first chapter of Genesis opens with these words, "In the beginning God created the heavens and the earth." The verse summarizes the drama that was about to unfold. We learn as we read on, that the earth was formless, empty, and dark, and God's Spirit moved over the waters preparing to carry out God's creative Word. And then God began to speak into existence his creation. A day by day account follows and on the penultimate day God created man, In His image, to commune with Him, fellowship with Him, enjoy Him. Man's destiny was to live in close fellowship with God forever. God took great delight in not just creating Adam and Eve but giving them dominion over the earth. Author Gene Edwards refers to this drama as The Divine Romance. Here we meet the creator of the universe unveiling the ultimate object of his love—man

It is interesting that all the verses up to day six talk about God in the singular ie. each verse says, 'And God said...' When it comes to the creation of man in verse 26 it says "Let Us [Father, Son and Holy Spirit] make mankind in Our image, after our likeness" The Father, Son and Holy Spirit, we call the Trinity, were in close fellowship with one another. They knew each other inside out and thought as One. Man was created out that incredibly intimate connection and fellowship. The Trinity's aim, plan and pleasure were that their relationship with man would mirror their relationship with each other. He was created out of love, for love and to love.

This week we are exploring the very first meal of the Bible, the apple in the Garden. Before they ate the apple Adam & Eve were living in unbroken fellowship with God. There was nothing hidden between them. Everything was laid bare (literally!). There was no shame, no question in their hearts about whether or not God loved them. They walked intimately with Him in the garden, exploring this incredible creation He had made for their enjoyment. Then one day they encountered the devil disguised as a serpent, and an unguarded and unwise conversation led to the first meal...

NOURISHED

—— DAY ONE ——

STORYLINE: GOD PLACED ADAM AND EVE IN A PLACE WHERE THEY COULD LIVE FULL. THEIR HUNGER WAS PERFECTLY MET EACH DAY AS THEY PARTNERED WITH GOD FOR THEIR WORTH. THEY WERE GIVEN WHAT THEY NEEDED.

Then God planted a garden in Eden, in the east. He put the Man He had just made in it. God made all kinds of trees grow from the ground, trees beautiful to look at and good to eat. The Tree-of-Life was in the middle of the garden, also the Tree-of-Knowledge-of-Good-and-Evil. **GENESIS 2:8–9 (MSG)**

THRIVE TO LIVE

Each of us were born with specific needs that must be met in order to keep us alive. When these needs are met, we can live full and wholehearted lives. If we neglect them we will live altered lives. Lives merely focused on survival...waking up each morning to cope, maintain, or just exist.

When Adam & Eve were in the garden with God they were thriving. Why? Because God was the one meeting all their needs.

Needs are not negotiable. They're not something we can put off until later or eventually get around to meeting. Needs are dominating. They are dictators of our human existence. Simply put, when our needs are met we live, but if we neglect them we die.

I remember when we were expecting our first son, Judah. We took a class about how to care for him. The presenter kept using the phrase, "Thrive to Live." We quickly learned that in order for him to live we needed to set up an environment for him to flourish in. If he thrived, he lived. The only guaranteed way for him to thrive was to make sure we met his needs.

Having needs doesn't make us needy. It makes us human. God is not afraid of us, nor is He afraid of the needs we have on a day-by-day, moment-by-moment basis. He's not surprised by them because He's the very One who put them within us. In His sovereignty He made us with needs. Our dependence on getting those needs met isn't a lack but, rather, proof of our need to connect to the One who created us. We were each made with two main areas of need:

EXTERNAL NEEDS

Firstly, our External Needs are the needs we have that are dependent upon environment and resources.

They keep us alive. Things like internet scrolling, retail therapy, eating chocolate in large quantities... Wait, I'm sorry; those just feel like needs! Our true basic human needs that must be met are food, water, sleep, oxygen and shelter. I think we all can agree that every human being deserves to have their basic needs met. In fact, we've built many humanitarian organizations and ministries throughout the world in an effort to ensure this. These needs can't be ignored, or people die. They are that important.

INTERNAL NEEDS

Our second set of needs are Internal Needs.

The primary internal need we have is to be LOVED. We have a deep desire to be loved for who we are. To be seen. The best way to describe this type of love is a desire to be enjoyed.

"We were created with a craving to be pursued, delighted in, and enjoyed, first by God and then by our loved ones. Understanding God's affection for us is where we begin to live exhilarated by His love." **MIKE BICKLE**

When we are deeply loved two specific things take place on the inside of us.

First, our Internal Need to be loved is met. We know we belong. Belonging means we are loved and accepted for who we are. When we are loved, it means we belong to someone. Every person, in order to live wholeheartedly, must know their worth and where they belong. When we have a deep sense of belonging, we feel accepted and loved for who we are. We feel at home. Nothing more. Nothing less. A human being. A human belonging.

Eden was a garden specifically planted by God. A place made perfect for Adam (and later, Eve) to occupy and dwell. Every square inch, tailor-made with them in mind; a vivid paradise created for them to flourish.

God invited Adam and Eve into the adventure of living with Him. They would walk with Him each day. Think about it ... they would walk and talk with the very One who made them. They resided in a permanent state of being fully loved and fully known. Living as they were intended to live. They belonged in Eden. They belonged to God. They were safe and secure in His care. God was meeting their primary internal needs from the beginning.

Secondly, our Internal Need for significance is met. We need to know we are worthy of attention. We need to know that we have value and are imperative to this world; that we can make a contribution. Our story of significance begins in our belonging. Once we know we belong, we begin to believe we have something to give, something to offer. Meaningful work comes from a sense of significance. Our life works when we acknowledge we belong to God. Our human story isn't as compelling as our heavenly belonging.

It was no different in the garden. The food was all around Adam and Eve. God designed an ecosystem that Adam would work the garden and feed himself. He didn't just have them fed. He wanted them to go through the process of feeding themselves, tending the land, working the garden and partnering with Him. Learning to feed yourself is part of living in God's garden. Everything you need is right in front of you, but He wants you to create just like Him. He understands your need to contribute and your need for importance. He loves it!

YOU ARE LOVED
Just like Adam and Eve, God deeply loves and enjoys you. He has from the very beginning.

"Long ago, even before He made the world, God loved us and chose us in Christ to be holy and without fault in His eyes. His unchanging plan has always been to adopt us into His own family by bringing us to Himself through Jesus Christ. And this gave Him great pleasure." **EPH. 1:4–5 (NLT)**

NEED IS A VERB
When we live with our basic needs met, we live FULL, not hungry.

But it's critical to note that these are continual ongoing needs that we must give attention to every day. Even the word 'Belong' in the Bible is a verb. It portrays a picture of us actively "ever becoming," and "belonging." It grows with us. It's not one meal. It's sitting at the table of a God who wants to meet our deepest need to belong and be significant on an ongoing basis. He's laid a feast for us but we often eat 'food' that does not nourish us or leaves us hungry. But we'll explore more of that tomorrow.

MAIN THOUGHTS TODAY
- Needs are given to us by God
- External needs keep us alive
- Internal needs allow us to thrive
- Our human story isn't as compelling as our heavenly belonging

ADD FIVE MINUTES TO YOUR STUDY
1. FOOD FOR THOUGHT

"God is most glorified in you when you are most satisfied in Him."
JOHN PIPER

Your desire to be loved is God-given. His love for you will be the only love that will never let you down, "never leave you, nor forsake you" and "nothing can separate you" from it. If you become acutely aware of it and fully immerse yourself in it, you will be 'full' and fully satisfied. Your pleasure in being loved by Him will bring Him the greatest glory.

2. THINGS TO 'CHEW' ON

Remembering that 'need' is an ongoing verb, think about your 'need' to be loved by God. Is it being fully met? Do you know in your heart that you are deeply, deeply loved?

_____

_____

_____

_____

_____

It's a humbling thing for us as humans to admit that we need to be loved. Our desire to be self-sufficient can be something that gradually comes between God and us and creates distance. For the length of this study, commit to taking time with Him daily to acknowledge your need for His love and to thank Him for it. Journal any changes to your relationship.

_____

_____

_____

_____

_____

WHISPERS

— DAY TWO —

STORYLINE: WE HAVE LEGITIMATE HUNGER IN OUR LIVES THAT THE ENEMY WILL USE AGAINST US, WHISPERING LIES. GOD LAYS A FEAST FOR US IN THE PRESENCE OF OUR ENEMY, IF WE WILL CHOOSE TO FEAST ON HIM.

The serpent was clever, more clever than any wild animal God had made. He spoke to the Woman: "Do I understand that God told you not to eat from any tree in the garden?" The Woman said to the serpent, "Not at all. We can eat from the trees in the garden. It's only about the tree in the middle of the garden that God said, 'Don't eat from it; don't even touch it or you'll die.'"
GENESIS 3:1–3 (MSG)

ENEMY OF YOUR SOUL

You have a real enemy of your soul: the devil. Your enemy was a created angel called Lucifer and used to be in heaven with God, enjoying close fellowship with Him. But he became obsessed with his own significance. He decided he would like to share God's glory and a mighty war broke out in heaven. He and a third of all the angels, who had sided with him, were cast to the earth. They became twisted and hell-bent on destroying those that God loves. We call them demons. The enemy's one goal; his main focus, is to drag you down with him. To fool you into believing God isn't as good as He said He is. To whisper to you that God will leave you hungry and that you will be left to fend for yourself, lacking.

It is a terrible lie, but this lie didn't start with your life. The enemy began this lie long before you existed. He came to your great grandmother Eve and lied to her. However, if you look closely at the passage above, you will see that he didn't come with an outright lie. He came with an over-statement that was deceitful and created doubt, curiosity and, eventually, compromise. Let's be clear; compromise will always leave us hungry. Eve ate the apple. When we eat the wrong meals, it leaves us dissatisfied, overwhelmed, hurt, full of regret and pain, ultimately hustling for our worth. Hustling for love.

THE TREE OF CHOICE

Adam and Eve knew what they needed to do to live. God gave them specific boundaries to keep them safe. The question I think we each ask is, "Why would God put a tree in the garden they shouldn't eat from?" Was God being mean? Was he baiting them? It's easy to think this way, but we have to look deeper. The tree represents choice. God, in His infinite wisdom, knows without being given a choice, we are powerless and therefore not free to choose to love. Without true choice there is no real love. It requires a choice to be authentic. The tree or, rather, the meal of the apple represents the power of choice. The moment we realize we are not forced to 'have to' and we move to 'want to,' everything changes. The joy comes! Real, genuine love is only expressed and enjoyed when we choose to say yes to one thing and say no to another.

"Why, then, did God give them free will? Because free will, though it makes evil possible, is also the only thing that makes possible any love or goodness or joy worth having." **CS LEWIS**

The enemy will most often take something God said and twist it. He will overstate it, exaggerate it, take it out of context. Always trying to trick you into feeding from the wrong source; eating the wrong 'meal'. He knows that you have authentic needs that must be 'fed', but he uses them against you. His goal is to leave you broken and dependent on the wrong thing, disconnected from the true source. Leaving you with an insatiable appetite to be loved.

LEGITIMATE NEED

The enemy will play on a legitimate need you have and offer you an illegitimate solution. Did Adam and Eve need to eat? Yes! So he was taking their need and redirecting their attention to another source. The danger comes when we don't know, or lose sight of, which table to eat at. We are hungry (legitimate), but we don't know where or how to get those needs met.

I remember the day I wanted to start being healthier. I spent the night before making promises to myself. Laying out my workout clothes, water bottle and setting my alarm. I woke up the next morning ready to go! I went to the gym, drank a green juice, and downed my liters of water. But life didn't stop. I had school pick ups, kids' homework, and dinner to make. Eventually, as the day went on I found myself wanting to eat, but I didn't have anything ready. I decided not to eat until I could make something healthy. The only problem is I didn't have anything prepared and I ended up with no time to prepare. At the end of the night, feeling utterly famished, I ate whatever I could find. It wasn't healthy and, guess what?

I went to bed feeling dissatisfied!

Most of us live lives where we want to eat the right things, but we are unprepared. We grin and bear it until we can't take it anymore and eat whatever we have in front of us. Many times we will go to bed feeling full but are left feeling disappointed, ashamed and full of regret.

We will tell ourselves we shouldn't have eaten, but we are challenging the wrong thing. The need and desire to eat is legitimate. If we allow it to be so, our focus can shift to eating the right things.

It reminds me of Psalm 23:5, "You prepare a table before me in the presence of my enemies." This passage tells us in the middle of any situation God can lay out the best food for us; the best sustenance. In fact, in The Message, it says, "You serve me a six course dinner..." We'll explore that more this week.

MAIN THOUGHTS TODAY
- Needs are legitimate
- The enemy offers us illegitimate solutions to them
- God offers a banquet
- We get to choose where we 'eat' from

ADD FIVE MINUTES TO YOUR STUDY
1. FOOD FOR THOUGHT

"How exquisite your love, O God! How eager we are to run under your wings. To eat our fill at the banquet you spread." **PSALM 36:7-8A (MSG)**

King David write most of the Psalms. Covenants, in the culture David lived in, were often concluded with a meal expressing the bond of friendship and protection. In Psalm 23:5 his Shepherd (God) was receiving King David at His table and placing him under His protection. The same invite goes out to us today when we are tempted and tormented by our enemy. To take cover under the shadow of His wings; to feast on His love and protection; to dwell in safety there.

2. THINGS TO 'CHEW' ON

"Be alert and sober of mind. Your enemy the devil prowls around like a roaring lion looking for someone to devour. Resist him..." **1PETER 5:8-9A**

We don't know how many times the serpent approached Eve or if it was even more than this one time. Maybe there were other moments she had resisted him. If so, perhaps her guard was down on this day. The devil is relentless in his pursuit of us, seeking to devour our faith and break our connection with God. Jesus experienced this in the desert. Have you? Think of a time when you felt 'taken out' by the enemy and ask the Holy Spirit to reveal where it started. Don't be surprised if you uncover a lie! Write the Truth down.

_____

_____

_____

_____

Continuing with the ongoing verb theme for a while. Consider that 'eating' is a continuous verb, too. In the natural, we need to eat meals regularly to survive. How much time in a day do you spend feasting at the Lord's table and enjoying the sustenance God offers, relying on His presence and His words to keep you full during the day? Journal your thoughts.

_____

_____

_____

_____

"My people... have abandoned Me, the spring of living waters; And instead, they have settled for dead and stagnant water from cracked, leaky cisterns of their own making." **JEREMIAH 2:13 (VOICE)**

God is saying here is that He is aware we drink (or, for the sake of this study, eat) from the wrong source. It's not a living source; it's stagnant, like eating old bread.

Take a moment and ask the Holy Spirit to show you a legitimate need you have that you are currently getting met from a stagnant source of your making. Is there a lie that the enemy whispered to you that caused you to create that source? Start a dialogue with the Lord about it, turn away from that source and ask Him how to start drinking and eating from His table.

_____

_____

_____

_____

EATING
——DAY THREE——

STORYLINE: EATING THE RIGHT FOOD IS DEPENDENT ON THE HEART WE HAVE TOWARDS GOD. WHEN WE KNOW WHO WE BELONG TO, OUR IDENTITY IS UNPARALLELED. DO WE LIVE AS SONS AND DAUGHTERS OR AS ORPHANS?

The serpent told the Woman, "You won't die. God knows that the moment you eat from that tree, you'll see what's really going on. You'll be just like God, knowing everything, ranging all the way from good to evil." When the Woman saw that the tree looked like good eating and realized what she would get out of it—she'd know everything!—she took and ate the fruit and then gave some to her husband, and he ate. **GENESIS 3:4-6 (MSG)**

CHILD OF GOD

I have four kids—four young sons. The day I became their mother, each of my boys had full access to me. It wasn't something I struggled to give them. The fact is, I wanted to give them everything I had. I wanted to hold them until they let go. I wanted to smother them with kisses and cuddles until their little love tanks were overflowing. And most of the time I did. The times when I felt like I had nothing more to give or struggled to help them was when I would bump up against my humanity. It simply came down to my capacity. My body couldn't always give what my heart was willing to provide.

You are a child of God. You're His kid, and this means you have access to everything He has. Unlike my clumsy and sometimes messy mothering, God is the perfect parent. He's good at what He does. He's been God for a long time (wink). He knows our every need. In fact, He can anticipate what we will need before we know we need it and is prepared to provide without fail.

The serpent came to Eve lying about God's parenting.

"The serpent told the Woman, "You won't die. God knows that the moment you eat from that tree, you'll see what's really going on. You'll be just like God, knowing everything, ranging all the way from good to evil."

Satan was right. Eve would know everything from good to bad. He was aware that once she ate the fruit, her innocence would be gone. She would be able to see all that was really going on. What she didn't realize is she would be breaking her connection with the only One who loved her without limits. A God who saw her as she was meant to be seen, and who thoroughly enjoyed her.

Eve believed a lie. The truth is that's all our enemy has: hatred, fear, and lies.

PLEASURABLE FOR A TIME

"When the Woman saw that the tree looked like good eating and realized what she would get out of it—she'd know everything!—she took and ate the fruit and then gave some to her husband, and he ate."

I think it's important to see here that Eve looked at the fruit. She saw it was good and what she would get out of it. The enemy will always lie to us about the outcome of getting our needs met his way. His primary aim is always, always to disconnect us from the Father. He sold rebellion to Eve and sugar coated it to look like innocent self-interest.

If the enemy's goal is always the same, why do we (like Eve) fall for his lies? It usually starts because we are living out of an orphan heart rather than a heart of sonship. What do I mean by this?

If we are living from an orphan heart, our primary narrative is, "I MUST get my needs met," and because we believe we are all alone and unloved, we feel we have to find our way to get those needs met. Dependency and trust are foreign to us. It speaks of being alone, abandoned and that the 'table' is not full. The enemy loves to help root those lies deeper into our hearts and will flash quick fixes in the face of an orphan heart. He knows we will 'sell our birthright for a bowl of soup' if we feel like there's nothing to lose. To an orphan, a meal (or a need met) is more important 'daily bread' to them than connection. The 'broken cisterns' they go to leave them feeling helpless, hopeless and ashamed, adding to their sense of being alone. Cycles of shame become their daily diet.

The heart of sonship says, "My Father loves me, knows me and will take care of me." It's grounded in trust that if I need it, it will come to me. If I don't have it, it's either not the right time or it's not good for me. Period. The heart of a son isn't looking for quick fixes or fast food; he knows His Father's table is full and abundant. He understands that connection to his Father is the most important resource he has. He can rest in the care and concern his Father has for him and is dependent on the connection as is his daily bread. He lives feeling seen, loved and knowing who he belongs to. His needs only remind him that his Father considers him worth providing for because he is worthy of the relationship.

At the moment that Eve opted to eat the fruit, she chose to live as an orphan even though all she had known up until that point was sonship. She forgot her identity. Eve wasn't trusting God's 'no'—she instead wanted a quick fix. She would know everything there was to know. But leaving the innocence of trust and dependency isn't all it's cracked up to be. Once you see, you can't unsee.

There are always consequences to living this way. When we don't live from a place of feeling loved, we don't live out of love. We will look at this tomorrow.

MAIN THOUGHTS TODAY
- Knowing who we belong to and our identity as sons is key to "eating right," naturally and spiritually
- An Orphan Heart lives adrift; from a place of lack, with daily bread of 'needs must be met'
- A Heart of Sonship lives in belonging; from trust with daily bread of 'connection is essential'
- Satan offers quick fixes and tempts us to sell our inheritance for a meal
- God provides the best, most nourishing meal!

ADD FIVE MINUTES TO YOUR STUDY
1. FOOD FOR THOUGHT

"Your words are so choice, so tasty; I prefer them to the best home cooking."
PSALM 119:103 (MSG)

There are a lot of food and eating analogies in the Bible; especially in Psalms and Proverbs. Mostly about 'eating' the words God speaks. Just pause for a moment and meditate on the verse quoted above. Consider it in the light of the study we have just done and your experience of enjoying good home cooking!

_____

_____

_____

2. THINGS TO 'CHEW' ON

"Whoever is poor and penniless can still come and buy the food I sell. There's no cost—here, have some food, hearty and delicious, and beverages, pure and good. I don't understand why you spend your money for things that don't nourish, or work so hard for what leaves you empty. Listen to Me and eat what is good; enjoy the richest, most delectable of things. Pay attention, come close now, listen carefully to my life-giving, life-nourishing words."
ISAIAH 55:1–3 (VOICE & MSG)

Listening and eating are the keywords in this verse. And in the original Hebrew of this verse they BOTH come from the same root word 'Qal,' meaning to listen, yield to, obey, consume, devour. So there is an activity of swallowing, digesting and chewing on (meditating) God's word to get all the nourishment out of it.

Is this how you read it or do you treat God's word like a fast food snack or an appetizer? Reflect on this and decide to read less and chew for longer. Journal what you discover when you do.

"It takes more than bread to stay alive. It takes a steady stream of words from God's mouth" **MATT 4:4 (MSG)**

Jesus' response to Satan, when tempted in the desert, was, "It takes more than bread to stay alive." He knew which table to eat at when in the presence of His enemy. Make a choice today to align yourself with Jesus' heart attitude towards the enemy when he tried to throw Him a quick fix and remember it when you are next faced with him trying to do the same to you.

"Open your mouth and taste, open your eyes and see—how good God is. Blessed are you who run to him. Worship God if you want the best; worship opens doors to all his goodness." **PSALM 34:8 (MSG)**

Here is a key to 'tasting'—worship opens the doors to the feast. Worship is singing praises, but it's also keeping a thankful and worshipful attitude at all times. Reflect on this area of your life and journal with the Lord.

_____

_____

_____

_____

_____

_____

_____

SHAME

— DAY FOUR —

STORYLINE: IF WE EAT AT THE ENEMY'S TABLE, WE FEEL SHAME AND WE HIDE. BUT SHAME IS AN OPPORTUNITY AND INVITATION TO RECONNECT WITH GOD; TO COME OUT OF HIDING AND SIT AT HIS TABLE AND EAT A NEW KIND OF FOOD.

"God created a good world that was subjected to futility because of the sinful, treasonous choice of the first human beings." **JOHN PIPER**

CHILDLIKE

Immediately, the two of them did "see what's really going on"—saw themselves naked! They sewed fig leaves together as makeshift clothes for themselves. When they heard the sound of God strolling in the garden in the evening breeze, the Man and his Wife hid in the trees of the garden; they hid from God. God called to the Man: "Where are you?" He said, "I heard you in the garden and I was afraid because I was naked. And I hid." 11 God said, "Who told you you were naked? Did you eat from that tree I told you not to eat from?"
GENESIS 3:7–11 (MSG)

It's hard to miss the horrifying picture we read above, and to understand what life suddenly felt like for Adam & Eve. To do so, you have to go back further in the story to get the full impact.

If you turn the page back, you'll see Genesis 2:25. It says here, "Adam and his wife were both naked, and they felt no shame." The Hebrew word for shame here is בּושׁ, 'boosh.' Boosh means to put to shame, to be ashamed, to be disappointed. Simply put, the Bible tells us that although Adam and Eve were naked, they felt no shame; they were not disappointed.

I think about my boys running around the house most days in capes and underwear. Thank God they're not old enough to notice that not everyone does this on a regular basis (or old enough to read this. Ha!). When I see them running around, my heart is full, and I want them to know two things.

First, I want them to know that they are enough. My sons don't need to be something they're not. The way they feel about their bodies is precisely how they were made to feel; free to be different. None of them comparing their body with any of their brothers or hiding in shame because they're not society's ideal. Each of them are God's ideal. Created by God; God's best idea. What each of them sees right now is enough for them to live happy, powerful and free.

Secondly, I want them to know that what God made is good. Their bodies, sexuality, and physical identity is tailor-made by God. Each boy was formed right in the middle of God's goodness. None of them ever have to question if he was a mistake, an afterthought, a quota. They don't have to live ashamed. They can enjoy their masculinity and the wild hearts God gave them. When God sees their form, He sees their goodness and He says, "That's my best idea!"

RESULT OF SIN

I'm not naive enough to believe they won't experience things differently as they grow up. It's impossible for our lives not to be touched by the result of sin. Shame is the result of sin. We have been born into a sinful world, and we are each sinful... Ok, don't freak out. Let me finish!

Think about this. Have you ever broken one of the ten commandments? Have you ever hurt someone? Ever done something wrong, even though you knew it was wrong? If you said yes—congratulations, you are human! We all have done things wrong and we will continue to do so. We are sinful. The results of our sin? We are each guilty, whether we feel guilty or not. We have all eaten the apple.

Were Adam and Eve guilty? Yes! Did they disobey and disbelieve what God had told them? Yes. And it resulted in shame. However, when shame is experienced, we do not need to stay there and hide. Shame can be turned to our advantage. Our shame can be an invitation to God. It can lead us back to Him; reminding us of our deep need for a Savior. He is the only one who can help us and 'feed' us something altogether more lovely.

SHAME ON DISPLAY

Biblical purity is about being free from guilt & shame. When God asked Adam & Eve where they were, Adam's response in verse 10 was, "I heard you in the garden, and I was afraid because I was naked. And I hid." The word naked here in the Hebrew is עֵירֹם `eyrom. It's a different root word than the word 'naked' used when they were walking with God. Eyrom means naked and helpless and ashamed. Adam and Eve went from living free and clear (like my boys running around) and without shame to feeling helpless and ashamed and hiding. It changed them.

When we eat from tables we were never intended to eat from, we are quickly left feeling helpless and ashamed, so we hide. We are embarrassed and pretend we didn't 'eat' that thing we knew we shouldn't have. This can move into feeling unlovable and unworthy. It might look satisfying, and/or be a quick fix, but it will leave us emotionally, spiritually and mentally bankrupt. We will no longer wonder what it feels like, smells like, and tastes like to be free and clear and intimately connected. Our bodies might be full, but our souls are left unsatisfied.

The enemy wants to put your SHAME ON DISPLAY and then he wants to keep you there. Helpless and hopeless. Naked. He loves the thought of you hiding from God. God is trying to call you out of hiding. He wants to reconnect with you again, quickly. One of the most compelling things we can learn about this moment with Adam & Eve is how God treats them. He was still looking for them, calling them. "Come out of hiding. You're not too naked for me to see you. I want to be with you!"

MAIN THOUGHTS TODAY
- They went from 'naked' to 'naked' but the second one involved shame
- Shame can be turned around into an opportunity to reconnect
- Sin, if admitted, turns into an invitation to sit at God's table and feast on intimacy
- We need not hide or feel ashamed of our need of God
- Repentance is a gift!

ADD FIVE MINUTES TO YOUR STUDY
1. FOOD FOR THOUGHT

"For the joy that was set before him [he] endured the cross, despising the shame" **HEBREWS 12:2**

This verse says that Jesus despised shame. What does this mean?
John Piper says the following: It means Jesus spoke to shame like this:

"Listen to me, Shame, do you see that joy in front of me? Compared to that, you are less than nothing. You are not worth comparing to that! I despise you. You think you have power. Compared to the joy before me, you have none. Joy. Joy. Joy. That is my power! Not you, Shame. You are worthless. You are powerless.

You think you can distract me. I won't even look at you. I have a joy set before me. Why would I look at you? You are ugly and despicable. And you are almost finished. You cover me now as with a shroud. Before you can say, 'So there!' I will throw you off like a filthy rag. I will put on my royal robe.

1. http://www.desiringgod.org/articles/what-does-it-mean-for-jesus-to-despise-shame

You think you are great, because even last night you made my disciples run away. You are a fool, Shame. You are a despicable fool. That abandonment, that loneliness, this cross — these tools of yours — they are all my sacred suffering, and will save my disciples, not desroy them. You are a fool. Your filthy hands fulfill holy prophecy.Farewell, Shame. It is finished."[1]

Jesus despised and destroyed shame and its ability to have power over you at the cross.

2. THINGS TO 'CHEW' ON

"People who conceal their sins will not prosper, but if they confess and turn from them, they will receive mercy." **PROVERBS 28:13 (NLT)**

Allow the truth of this verse to sink in. Consider what benefit it is to you to pretend you didn't 'eat the fruit.' According to this verse, there is no benefit. In fact, it will harm you. The alternative is to hold your head up, admit it, turn away, and you will receive and experience compassion and mercy. Take a moment to ask the Holy Spirit if there are things you haven't admitted to that are harming you. Confess them and turn away from them.

"Look on me with a heart of mercy, O God, according to Your generous love. According to Your great compassion, wipe out every consequence of my shameful crimes. Thoroughly wash me, inside and out, of all my crooked deeds. Cleanse me from my sins. For I am fully aware of all I have done wrong, and my guilt is there, staring me in the face. It was against You, only You, that I sinned, for I have done what You say is wrong, right before Your eyes... Create in me a clean heart, O God; restore within me a sense of being brand new". **PSALM 51:1–4+10 (VOICE)**

David wrote Psalm 51 after he committed adultery with Bathsheba. There is no emotional hiding evident in this Psalm; neither is there any self-justification. He holds his hands up and acknowledges, 'I ate the fruit!' Take a moment to ponder his honesty and frankness as he faces God. How will this change your temptation to hide next time you 'eat from the wrong table?

"But if we own up to our sins, God shows that He is faithful and just by forgiving us of our sins and purifying us from the pollution of all the bad things we have done." **1 JOHN 1:9 (VOICE)**

Further on in Psalm 51 King David cries to God to cleanse him and make him whole according to His great faithfulness. Here in 1 John 1, this characteristic of God's nature is stated once again. We know it to be true because of the outcome of David's life and God's generosity towards him. How is your faith in God's forgiveness and purifying ability strengthened by the story of David?

COVERED

— DAY FIVE —

STORYLINE: GOD'S LOVE AND CONCERN COVERED THEM WHEN THEY HAD JUST BLOWN IT BIG TIME. IN YOUR SHAME HE COVERS YOU AND ALREADY HAS A PLAN FOR REDEMPTION.

"God made leather clothing for Adam and his wife and dressed them."
GENESIS 3:21.

CHILD OF GOD
HIDING

Helpless, naked and ashamed. Can you just picture Adam & Eve in the garden? Their innocence stripped from them. Their eyes opened, and their souls violated in a moment. One minute they are basking in the delight of this paradise, fully loved, fully known and, in the next, they are thrown into the knowledge of good and evil. They see the world differently.

There was a commercial on TV a few years ago. The beginning scene is a beautiful little girl with big blue eyes and fair skin, celebrating her birthday. She's holding a cake in front of her with all the candles lit. People are all around, and her face is full of life. As they begin to zoom in on her face, the scene starts changing and you see her going about a typical day in her UK life. Half way through the video everything changes as you see the environment around her shift into a war zone. Her face gradually gets dirtier. You see her going from a vibrant room full of family and friends, into a war-torn community where she's running for her life. Immediately you are pulled into the reality of her life. She's still a little girl. Something about this moment draws you in because you realize she deserves what every kid deserves, love, security, and safety. And yet at the end of the video she's in a place of danger, terrified and alone.

When I read Genesis 3, I reflect on this picture. It's as if Adam and Eve are the innocent little girl. They don't know dark things: abuse, rape, neglect, abandonment, pure evil. They only know good things. Suddenly they are thrown into a war zone, the war between Heaven and Earth, the devil, and God. They now see what God was trying to protect them from, but it's too late. Their innocence is out of reach. Their confidence is shattered. They are hiding because they were afraid.

CLEAN

God calls them. They answer. Their bellies are full, but their souls are empty because of self-indulgence. It's quickly evident they are not the same. The morning after has left them looking for clothes. Anything to get rid of the stench of shame.

My Dad used to share a story about a woman who was living in their community of believers. She had lived a life on the streets, selling her body for money. Selling her soul. One day, they noticed she had been in the shower for a long time. They went to check on her, asking her what was going on. Through sobs, she blurted out, "I'm trying to get clean." It was evident the dirt and filth were on the inside of her. No amount of showering or soap was going to leave her feeling completely clean no matter how long she scrubbed.

Just like this woman, no amount of clothing was going to hide Adam and Eve's shame. They were ashamed and helpless on the inside. No amount of hiding was going to remedy how exposed they felt.

"We please Him most, not by frantically trying to make ourselves good, but by throwing ourselves into His arms with all our imperfections and believe that He understands everything—and still loves us." **A.W. TOZER**

The most beautiful part of this creation story comes next. If you don't look for it, you might miss it. It says, "God made leather clothing for Adam and his wife and dressed them." Even in the midst of their shame, fear, and awareness, God was still their protector. Right in front of their eyes, He makes them clothes.

PROTECTED

It's as if a Dad walked in to see his daughter in an intimate position with another man. She is naked. The truth about her life is laid bare in front of him. But instead of shaming her, leaving her in a mess, he takes a robe and covers her. He can't help but protect her. His love is far greater than her actions. The desire to cover, protect and provide, overrides any other motive.

Even though Adam and Eve's bellies were full with apples, the wrong kind of meal, God was already preparing another meal. A meal that would heal all humanity and satisfy even their deepest hunger for love. The ingredients of this meal would cost God more than Adam and Eve could ever comprehend.

MAIN THOUGHTS TODAY
- You were born out of love, for love and to love
- Your need for love is valid
- In your shame, He covers you with love and protection
- He says, "Come as you are" and welcomes you
- When we let Him down, He is already making a plan of rescue and redemption

ADD FIVE MINUTES TO YOUR STUDY
1. FOOD FOR THOUGHT

"We please Him most, not by frantically trying to make ourselves good, but by throwing ourselves into His arms with all our imperfections and believe that He understands everything—and still loves us." **A.W.TOZER**

Meditate on this quote for a minute. How is your faith to believe this? Do you run into His open arms every time you let Him down, or do you hide?

2. THINGS TO 'CHEW' ON

*"But you'll welcome us with open arms when we run for cover to you.
Let the party last all night! Stand guard over our celebration. You are
famous, God, for welcoming God-seekers, for decking us out in delight."*
PSALM 5:11–12 (MSG)

Allow the truth of this incredible verse to sink in. God covers you; He is
your hiding place and strong tower of refuge in times of trouble. To hide
from Him is of no benefit to you. He sees and knows everything, and
there is no judgment in His heart towards you. In fact, it will harm you
further if you can't hear His voice or feel His presence while at your most
vulnerable. Commit to keeping a very short account with Him. Journal
your thoughts.

*"When I finally saw my own lies, I owned up to my sins before You, and I did
not try to hide my evil deeds from You. I said to myself, "I'll admit all my sins
to the Eternal," and You lifted and carried away the guilt of my sin."*
PSALM 5:11–12 (MSG)

We can lie to ourselves and to God and justify our sin because we are
ashamed. Then we feel burdened. God wants to lift all of that off us
quickly and immediately, but we have to confess and acknowledge. Take
a moment and ask the Holy Spirit to help you and nudge you when
you're hiding.

_____

_____

_____

_____

_____

_____

_____

_____

_____

_____

_____

_____

_____

_____

BREAD +WINE

HUNGER TO BELONG

"When you get to a place where you understand that love and belonging, your worthiness, is a birthright and not something you have to earn, anything is possible."

BRENÉ BROWN

When you experience problems in your life, what do you typically do? Who do you usually call or need to see? We all need to feel accepted and supported by others to keep us from feeling lonely, anxious or depressed. When we can build strong connections with others, it helps us greatly in coping with distressing situations.

From a psychological perspective, a sense of belonging goes back to infancy. In fact, it is so powerful, that without a sense of belonging we never learn healthy coping mechanisms when experiencing intense and painful emotions. Not only that, but it can impact our social skills, intellectual capability, and our mental and physical health, too, causing depression, anxiety and a lack of direction in life.

From the moment we are born, we are asking the questions 'Who am I? Where do I belong and who do I belong to?' A young baby will cry and cry for their mother, needing constant reassurance of closeness and belonging. Children at an early age begin to form little groups at school. Typically they orbit around their enjoyment of the same activities or live in proximity to each other. Friendships begin. As the child moves into teenage years, they become aware of fashion, and a massive shift takes place. Things like what they wear, the kind of music they listen to, and the places they hang out all start to give a sense of belonging. Kids are often bullied at school if they stand out in any way or are different, so a lot of them adapt to fit in and 'belong.' We all remember the 'popular' boys and girls at school—everybody wanted to be like them. They begin to conform to their peers. They hide their true self, their opinions, and tastes, for fear of being rejected. By the time they reach adulthood some will have forgotten they've taught themselves to do this. They will no longer remember how much of how they are as an adult is the 'real' them and how much is a learned behavior. We get married and have children. Our houses and cars need to fit in so that we belong to whichever social group we associate our belonging. We join clubs. We frequent gyms and go to classes because we want to belong to someone or a group of someones. Perhaps our greatest fear of all is to be alone or rejected.

Sometimes all we need to know is "we are not alone." It's why Jesus came to die because He couldn't be everywhere and with everyone at once. That's why He said to His disciples, "But I tell you, it is for your good that I am going away. Unless I go away, the Advocate will not come to you." He knew that the new plan that God had made involved Him (His Holy Spirit) coming to dwell in people's hearts. THAT was going to be His new temple. Us! The original Greek word for Advocate here is parakletos, the Helper; the one who comes alongside, who comes to your aid and pleads your case. Holy Spirit is also called Counselor and Comforter. He can help us navigate challenging and troubling times, and we are never alone. How awesome is that!

God is not all we need(stay with me, I know we sing that!) If that were truth then back in the beginning when Adam was formed in the Garden of Eden and was in perfect relationship with the Trinity, God would not have said: "It is not good for the man to be alone." He then made Eve as a companion for Adam. Belonging and community are intertwined, and this is the reason why God loves the church. He doesn't just love and enjoy us getting together to praise Him and learn about Him. He LOVES it when we fellowship together, hang out, sharing our lives and possessions. It's what Jesus modeled to the disciples and what the early church in Acts did.

So our hunger to belong and our sense of belonging are critical to our soul. Come with me into Week Two where we explore this desire and God's remedy.

ANOTHER MEAL

—— DAY SIX ——

STORYLINE: ADAM & EVE'S CHOICE SEPARATED US ALL FROM GOD BUT HE HAD ALREADY PLANNED ANOTHER MEAL TO REVERSE THE EFFECTS OF THE FIRST MEAL.

"The days are coming," declares the Lord, "when I will make a new covenant..."
JEREMIAH 31:31

NOT GOOD ENOUGH

There was a remedy to this global drama gone wrong, but God's eternal plan was going to unfold over the next two thousand years. It wasn't a quick fix. It was the most elaborate, selfless and passionate love story ever told and it was going to take another meal to reverse the effects of the first meal.

The reality of what Eve and Adam set in motion was a helpless and hopeless outcome. Now touched with evil, it didn't take long for the enemy's purpose to prevail over them. Once the enemy has full control, he goes to work destroying any sign of life. Their story reeked of selfishness, hostility, and hopelessness.

Adam and Eve didn't have an answer to solve the sin problem, which means you and I don't have an answer either. Our destiny forever linked to their fate. Adam and Eve were guilty of sin. They knew evil, and now every human born on the earth would know that same evil and be sinful. The fact was simple. We could no longer live with a perfect God for eternity as rebellious people. God is perfect and holy, and that's His environment. It is not possible for a holy God to be in a relationship with unholy people. It doesn't matter how we have cleaned ourselves up or how many good things we do; nothing can take away the sin we each have. No amount of good works can outdo the goodness of God in paying the ultimate price to restore us. And because sin entered our lives, we deserve to spend eternity with our enemy. Adam and Eve's choice to trust the enemy over God (their sin) determined an eternal hell for us, away from God; away from His love. It was a hopeless case. Our sin keeps us from God, but we still need Him.

The only way for the price of our sin to be paid was a living sacrifice of an animal without defect, according to the Old Testament. For the redemption of humanity, it was going to be The Lamb without defect: the Son of God. Sin results in separation from God. We deserve death. We deserve hell. But God...God was making a way where there was no way. His plan? Clear. He would send His only Son to die on our behalf; to take the punishment that we deserved for our personal sin. An innocent God, would come in human form, live a sinless life and then take the penalty for our sins. He would die a horrific death, piled with all our sin and experience (for the first time in His life) the wrath of God, so that we could be spared. And that's not all; He would do this for any and everyone who wanted to reconnect to Him; to belong to Him. Those who wanted to live in eternity with Him. In fact, the whole world was invited into this redemptive plan. He would pay the price we all deserved. God would do what no man could do for himself: save his soul.

Fast forward 2,000 years.

THE LAST SUPPER
We find God has come to earth. Jesus, Emmanuel, God with us. Jesus has lived for 33 years, the last three of those being ministry years, gathering 12 disciples around Him; training them in the ways of God and the gospel. The future leaders of the First Church.

Today we are going to take a look at that momentous time in Scripture where Jesus is about to have his last meal with his disciples. Each of them was unaware that His time is coming to an end. The preparations are already in motion, but the disciples have no idea what's in store for the next three days. Jesus instructs them to prepare a place for them where they can host the Passover Meal, a traditional Jewish supper.

On the first of the Days of Unleavened Bread, the day they prepare the Passover sacrifice, his disciples asked him, "Where do you want us to go and make preparations so you can eat the Passover meal?" He directed two of his disciples, "Go into the city. A man carrying a water jug will meet you. Follow him. Ask the owner of whichever house he enters, 'The Teacher wants to know, Where is my guest room where I can eat the Passover meal with my disciples?' He will show you a spacious second-story room, swept and ready. Prepare for us there." The disciples left, came to the city, found everything just as he had told them, and prepared the Passover meal. **MARK 14:12–16 (MSG)**

I love this side of Jesus. He's prophetic! He tells them exactly what is going to happen and it does. They think they are following tradition, but God is changing history.

PREPARING A MEAL

We can find hope at this very moment. Whatever you're going through right now God is preparing a miracle. There are times when God tells us to go and do something, and it can seem crazy. We can try and make sense of it, but God is setting up our defense. Our only responsibility is to listen to the truth and obey.

I can think back to the moment in my life where I felt like everything was falling apart. I had given birth to our fourth son. It was my fourth C-section in five years. I was exhausted. Struggling with postpartum depression, I was under a dark cloud of life. Our littlest was in the NICU for ten days, and I came home to find all my other boys had hand, foot & mouth disease, quarantined for another ten days. Just when I thought I was coming up for air, I received a phone call from my husband. The church we worked for during the last 15 years was letting us go due to financial troubles. I hung up the phone and went into my bedroom to have an adult tantrum. I fell on the bed without my arms and began to sob, telling God I didn't know what He wanted me to do. I felt at the end of my rope. I gently heard Him say, "I want you to make chicken." I thought... WHAT! And I responded, "You make chicken." Crying and laughing at the same time. I felt Him encouraging me to get up and make the meal. Eventually, I told myself, "Well, I have nothing better to do. I might as well obey God." I didn't feel like a person of faith in that moment. But I picked myself up, washed my face and made a chicken dinner. It's hard to explain, but at that moment everything shifted. Once I was willing to get up and make chicken, I felt hope in my heart. The meal changed everything even when nothing in the physical had changed. God initiated a conversation with me about a meal and in turn it activated hope in me that God knew what was going on and had a plan.

The disciples thought they were setting up for just another meal, but God was setting up a heavenly exchange. He was turning it all around. They didn't have the power to make anything happen but they could prepare a meal to host divine destiny.

Today you may be faced with the impossible. Life circumstances may feel like they are trapping you. You have been asking God, "What should I do?" Do the very thing in front of you. Wash your face, do the dishes, send the email, call the friend. Do the last thing God told you to do. Often it's in the mundane that He's working a miracle.

MAIN THOUGHTS TODAY
- Adam & Eve's choice separated us all from God
- BUT God had planned another meal to reverse the effect of the first meal
- Jesus took the punishment that was yours, to reconcile you back with God
- When you feel overwhelmed, He is working miracles on your behalf

ADD FIVE MINUTES TO YOUR STUDY

1. FOOD FOR THOUGHT

"Do not be afraid, Daniel. From the very first day that you began to pursue understanding and humble yourself before your God, your words have been heard. I have been sent in response to what you've said. 13 I would have been here sooner; however, for the past 21 days the spirit prince of Persia opposed me and prevented my coming to you. Then Michael, one of the chief princes of heaven, came to my aid.." **DANIEL 10:12-13 (MSG)**

From the moment Daniel started praying, angels were dispatched to answer him, but there was opposition in the spirit realm. Whatever you are facing, keep coming to God. "Don't fret or worry. Instead of worrying, pray. Let petitions and praises shape your worries into prayers, letting God know your concerns. Before you know it, a sense of God's whole-ness, everything coming together for good, will come and settle you down."[2] The answer will come. While you are feeling overwhelmed He is working things out and we can be confident because, "we know that God causes everything to work together for the good of those who love God"... and that includes you!

2. THINGS TO 'CHEW' ON

"Jesus became a priest, not by meeting the physical requirement of belonging to the tribe of Levi, but by the power of a life that cannot be destroyed." **HE-BREWS 7:16 (NLT)**

"Such a high priest truly meets our need—one who is holy, blameless, pure, set apart from sinners, exalted above the heavens. Unlike the other high priests, he does not need to offer sacrifices day after day, first for his own sins, and then for the sins of the people. He sacrificed for their sins once for all when he offered himself." **HEBREWS 7:26-27**

There is much value in reading the Old Testament. The whole book of Leviticus is dedicated to the 'do's' and 'don'ts' for the Israelite nation and describes the different sacrifices the priests constantly had to make for the Israelites. These sacrifices were to atone for their sins of the people and meet the holy requirements of God. Whole days were set aside for

2. Philippians 4:6-7 (MSG)

ceremonial cleansing and slaughtering and it was an expensive business! Even then they didn't get a direct connection with God; He only spoke to them through the prophets. Reading the Old Testament reminds us of the work of the cross and what Jesus did for us.

Take a moment to journal your thanks to God for the new plan of sending Jesus. He paid once and for all; done deal. It means you don't have to jump through all these hoops for a third party connection. You get direct access to God. You have direct access to the holy of holies.

BELONGING TO A FATHER

—— DAY SEVEN ——

STORYLINE: GOD IS A LOVING, FORGIVING FATHER WHO RUNS TOWARDS US WHEN WE HAVE MESSED UP AND RESTORES US BACK TO HIMSELF, LAVISHING US WITH GRACE, MERCY AND FORGIVENESS.

"I am the prodigal son every time I search for unconditional love where it cannot be found." **HENRI J.M. NOUWEN, RETURN OF THE PRODIGAL SON**

SQUANDERED INHERITANCE

Imagine the story of a billionaire's son. He lived in the middle of New York City in a big and fabulous penthouse. His father was a well loved and respected philanthropist. He made most of his wealth in the real estate market. From a young age, he learned how to buy and sell. He starting with a small corner convenience store and eventually sold some of the most sought after estates on the market. His success was known far and wide. Eventually, as they grew, both his sons began to work for him.

The billionaire wasn't like many of his colleagues, offering corner offices to their offspring. He started the boys from the ground up: mailrooms, lunch deliveries, internships. After all, there was so much to do, and he wanted them to experience every facet of his business. Always watching to see if one of his boys had his instincts. He knew some things could only be "caught," not "taught," and his eldest son was in line to take over the family business, as planned.

Everything was moving forward until someone from the accounting department caught his youngest son stealing from the enterprise. At first, it seemed it was a small discrepancy, but with further investigation it was devastating. The young man was hiding a decade of gambling debts. He had been moving money around, covering his lifestyle and stealing from his father's lifetime of wealth and reputation. When his father went to confront him, his son said, "What does it matter? All this is mine, regardless?" The father was struck by the son's lack of character. He felt he was entitled to all his father had worked so hard to build. The son had no regard, respect or honor for his Dad. It was all about him. His needs took urgent priority, but in reality, it stole his dignity, trust and, ultimately, his relationship with his father.

In Luke 15, we find a Bible story much like the one above. A wealthy Dad was willing to give all he owned to his kids. The only hindrance? Timing. The boys would need to work, prepare and wait for their inheritance; that was the natural order of things. Suddenly, out of nowhere, the youngest son demands his share of the estate. The Bible says he came to his Dad and said, "Give me my money" and the father grants his wish.

We learn quickly that the son spent his money on a lavish lifestyle. Eventually, he squandered everything he'd received and was rendered broke, hungry, and desperate. The son devised a plan to go back to his father's house. He decided that even if he had to work as a servant there, he would be better off than where he was that day.

A SON RESTORED

As the son made his way home, his Dad saw him from a long way off and ran to him. He was filled with compassion for him, embraced him and kissed him. Clothing him in the best robe, he put a ring on his finger, sandals on his feet and called for a fattened calf to be slaughtered In celebration. His long lost son was HOME!!!

We know this story in the Bible as The Prodigal Son, but in the Middle Eastern church, the story goes by another name: The Story of the Running Father. What a beautiful picture!

OUR STORY

His story is our story too. We have a Father in Heaven. He knows we have squandered our eternal lives. Humanity has chosen to go its own way. Our path is full of sin and shame. In our darkness, He comes running. Not as a Father embarrassed by a rebellious son. Not as a Dad coming to lecture his prodigal child, shaming him back home. No! He comes running towards us when we are still a long way off, not expecting full restoration. The salvation story is about a running Father.

But God clearly shows and proves His love for us, by the fact that while we were still sinners, Christ died for us. **ROMANS 5:8 (AMP)**

Even while we are walking the walk of shame, God has a plan. He is working it out. Even when we can't help ourselves, the Father is in a full sprint toward us. He wants to bring us into His house, clothe us with righteousness, put a ring on us and throw a feast.

The Last Supper was the beginning of a celebration. It was the end and the beginning. Jesus was going to die a gruesome death. A death he didn't deserve. It looked like the end of a man claiming to be the Messiah, but it was the beginning of God providing His new plan of salvation. The wheels were in motion!

Why would God devise such a plan? We belong to Him. He gives us meaning. We are His creation, made in His image, and He wants us to be with Him. After all is said and done, God is still a Father, and we are His children. He loves us fully and desperately. We are His reward.

MAIN THOUGHTS TODAY
• God is our Father
• He is the Father who runs towards us when we have messed up
• He celebrates us when we return; clothing us and preparing a feast
• We belong to Him; we are made to be with Him

ADD FIVE MINUTES TO YOUR STUDY
1. FOOD FOR THOUGHT

"...let us run with perseverance the race marked out for us. Let us fix our eyes on Jesus, the author and perfecter of our faith, who for the joy set before him endured the cross". **HEBREWS 12:1-2**

He is the Father who runs unrestrained towards us with fierce love and unending forgiveness and mercy. He can do this because of the sacrifice of Jesus. These verses say 'for the joy set before Him.' It wasn't just the joy of being reunited with His Father that caused Him to endure the cross; it was for the pleasure of knowing you and joining you back to the Father; reconnecting you with Him the way you were always meant to be.

2. THINGS TO 'CHEW' ON

"I have revealed you to the ones you gave me from this world. They were always yours. You gave them to me, and they have kept your word. Now they know that everything I have is a gift from you, for I have passed on to them the message you gave me. They accepted it and know that I came from you, and they believe you sent me."My prayer is not for the world, but for those you have given me, because they belong to you. All who are mine belong to you, and you have given them to me, so they bring me glory" **JOHN 17:6-10**[3]

---

3 Emphasis is mine.

Jesus' last prayer on earth before being arrested, tried and crucified is John 17. The tone of it is intimate, and the sole focus of His prayer was for those that the Father had given him; his disciples and all those of us in the future who would believe in Him. He didn't pray for the world, He prayed first and foremost for them and us because we're His; we belong to Him and the Father, and He treasured us. Take a few minutes to consider that Jesus looked down through the ages and had you in mind when He prayed this. Jesus knew you then and prayed for you because you belong to the Father.

_____

_____

_____

_____

_____

_____

"But when the time arrived that was set by God the Father, God sent his Son, born among us of a woman, born under the conditions of the law so that he might redeem those of us who have been kidnapped by the law. Thus we have been set free to experience our rightful heritage. You can tell for sure that you are now fully adopted as his own children because God sent the Spirit of his Son into our lives crying out, "Papa! Father!" Doesn't that privilege of intimate conversation with God make it plain that you are not a slave, but a child?" **GALATIANS 4:6–7 (MSG)**

It's a done deal; your Father has officially adopted you in Heaven! Take some time to think about what it means to be childlike (not childish!) with a Father who is never going to leave you nor forsake you and who has all the resources of Heaven at His fingertips!

_____

_____

_____

_____

_____

_____

_____

_____

BELONGING TO A SAVIOR

— DAY EIGHT —

STORYLINE: THE LAST SUPPER WAS A PIVOTAL MOMENT IN GOD'S NEW PLAN BECAUSE JESUS USED IT TO SYMBOLIZE WHAT WAS ABOUT TO HAPPEN IN ORDER FOR MAN TO BE RECONCILED TO GOD.

"The great thing to remember is that, though our feelings come and go, His love for us does not. It is not wearied by our sins, or our indifference; and, therefore, it is quite relentless in its determination that we shall be cured of those sins, at whatever cost to us, at whatever cost to Him."
C.S. LEWIS—MERE CHRISTIANITY

LAST MEAL TOGETHER

Jesus and His disciples are having their last meal together. Can you imagine? The disciples think they are just having a meal, but Jesus knows everything is about to change. Remember, Jesus is fully God, but He is also fully man. Everything He would have experienced is exactly how we would have experienced it, too.

The time had come for the world to change. Jesus was going to be crucified. I love how Jesus uses food to help symbolize and bring to life what He was about to do. He explains this is His last meal until His mission to save the world is over.

When it was time, he sat down, all the apostles with him, and said, "You've no idea how much I have looked forward to eating this Passover meal with you before I enter my time of suffering. It's the last one I'll eat until we all eat it together in the kingdom of God." **LUKE 22:14-16 (MSG)**

BREAD & WINE

Jesus takes them through an object lesson. Giving them food for thought... no pun intended... ok, just a little... He grabs the wine and the bread, beginning to explain what it symbolizes. Taking it, passing it, unearthing its mystery.

Taking the cup, he blessed it, then said, "Take this and pass it among you. As for me, I'll not drink wine again until the kingdom of God arrives." Taking bread, he blessed it, broke it, and gave it to them, saying, "This is my body, given for you. Eat it in my memory." He did the same with the cup after supper, saying, "This cup is the new covenant written in my blood; blood poured out for you." **LUKE 22:18–20**

I'll never forget the first time I took communion. I was seven years old, and we were on a ministry trip to England. My dad was a traveling preacher. The picture of him preaching the gospel in a church with wooden pews is still clear to this day. I remember him talking about the price Jesus paid for our sins. He was describing His agonizing death. His words gripped my heart, and I began to cry. I was having a moment of realization. I was undeserving of such great love and great sacrifice, yet He had still saved me. He invited me to take communion that day, and I cried as I took each part of the bread and wine. From that day forward communion meant something to me. The revelation I had received brought ownership; this now really was my story. Jesus was my Savior. His blood shed, and His body broken, for me.

This passage clearly shows why we take communion in our church communities. It's to remember what Christ did that day at Calvary. But we don't do it just to remember, we also do it to bring our hearts, minds, souls and spirits into alignment with Him. It's a time when we take the elements of this meal and declare, "I'm united with Christ. I belong to Him and nothing can ever separate me from His love."

Chew on the bread that gives life, and you will never be hungry. Drink of the wine that never runs out and your thirst will be quenched. It's a time to savor. To reflect on the price God gave so that we could be with Him. A meal that remedied the fall of man.

"This is how much God loved the world: He gave his Son, his one and only Son. And this is why: so that no one need be destroyed; by believing in him, anyone can have a whole and lasting life. God didn't go to all the trouble of sending his Son merely to point an accusing finger, telling the world how bad it was. He came to help, to put the world right again. Anyone who trusts in him is acquitted; anyone who refuses to trust him has long since been under the death sentence without knowing it. And why? Because of that person's failure to believe in the one-of-a-kind Son of God when introduced to him." **JOHN 3:16–18 (MSG)**

I have made it a regular practice to take communion. I need to be reminded over and over again what Jesus did for me that day. I encourage you to do the same.

MAIN THOUGHTS TODAY
- The Last Supper was a pivotal moment in God's new plan
- Communion is about remembrance, symbolism & alignment
- His body broken, and His blood poured out, so that you could belong
- Eating and drinking of God will feed you and quench your thirst

ADD FIVE MINUTES TO YOUR STUDY
1. FOOD FOR THOUGHT

"While others are congratulating themselves, I have to sit humbly at the foot of the cross and marvel that I'm saved at all." **C.H.SPURGEON**

A grateful heart is a humble heart, and a humble heart is a heart like Jesus. Let's never forget what an incredible, incredible privilege it is to know the King of Kings. Let's never take for granted the full access we have to Heaven and conversation with God because of what Jesus did. He is our Savior, and we belong to Him.

2. THINGS TO 'CHEW' ON

"...let us run with perseverance the race marked out for us. Let us fix our eyes on Jesus, the author and perfecter of our faith, who for the joy set before him endured the cross." **HEBREWS 12:1-2**

He is the Savior who runs unrestrained towards us with fierce love and unending forgiveness and mercy. He can do this because He made the perfect sacrifice. These verses say 'for the joy set before Him.' It wasn't just the joy of being reunited with His Father that caused Him to endure the cross; it was for the pleasure of knowing you and joining you back to the Father; reconnecting you with Him the way you were always meant to be. It was the love of the Father that sent the Son, and you belong to them both.

_____

_____

_____

_____

_____

_____

_____

_____

_____

_____

BELONGING TO HEAVEN
— DAY NINE —

STORYLINE: HEAVEN IS REALLY THE PLACE WHERE WE BELONG; OUR TRUE HOME.

"The fact that our hearts yearn for something earth can't supply is proof that Heaven must be our home." **C.S.LEWIS**

OUR BELONGING

Belonging comes when we realize Whose we are. Over the last couple of days, we've looked at our history with Adam & Eve and touched on our belonging to the Father and the Son (our Savior).

As we've explored, we've seen that we belong to the Godhead—the Trinity. The Bible clearly speaks of: God the Son, God the Father, and God the Holy Spirit but emphasizes that there is only ONE God.

"Thus the term: "Tri" meaning three, and "Unity" meaning one, Tri+Unity = Trinity. It is a way of acknowledging what the Bible reveals to us about God, that God is yet three "Persons" who have the same essence of deity. Some have tried to give human illustrations for the Trinity, such as H2O being water, ice and steam (all different forms, but all are H2O). Another illustration would be the sun. From it we receive light, heat and radiation. Three distinct aspects, but only one sun."[4]

It reminds me of living in my home. On any given day my husband Ben can be called Dad, husband or son. None of these are wrong. He is all of these things at the same time. It's the same with the Names of God. We can call Him Father, Jesus, or Holy Spirit. He is Three in One. Most importantly, these Names ground us in our belonging. Our needs are changeable, but He remains consistent and available. When we need a Father, we have one. When we need a Savior, He is there. When we need guidance, reassurance, power and the tangible presence of God, the Holy Spirit is ever present, living within us.

4 http://www.everystudent.com/forum/trinity.html

God lives in heaven. God is heaven. Heaven is our home.

HOMESICK

Today I want us to look at our Heavenly belonging. The Bible clearly tells us our real home is in heaven. God has a city waiting for us.

Each one of these people of faith died not yet having in hand what was promised, but still believing. How did they do it? They saw it way off in the distance, waved their greeting, and accepted the fact that they were transients in this world. People who live this way make it plain that they are looking for their true home. If they were homesick for the old country, they could have gone back any time they wanted. But they were after a far better country than that—heaven country. You can see why God is so proud of them, and has a City waiting for them. Hebrews 11:13–16 (MSG)

As a family, we have the opportunity of traveling to minister, and sometimes those travels take us to other countries. Honestly, I love to be on the go! I grew up on the road, so going places, exploring new environments, and meeting new people is one of my favorite things on the planet. But even when everything is going just as planned, there is always a moment on every trip when I miss home. I miss the familiarity of my environment; the place I do life. Eventually, we make our way back, and my favorite thing to do is run outside, take my shoes off, and walk barefoot in the yard. I love being home! In fact, I forget how much my home is truly me. Once I'm through the door, I deeply inhale my space. I belong there.

Billy Graham said, "My home is in heaven. I'm just traveling through this world."

What a true statement. You are made for another place; free from pain, heartache, abuse and sickness. Understanding this truth helps us give ourselves compassion. Grace to live in a world that is not home. Let me ask you a question. Have you ever felt off? Even when everything is going as planned, do you have a deep longing? I believe our hunger and desire come from our heavenly citizenship.

It also gives us permission to invest in our heavenly home. We can live for things Heaven rewards; not just for an earthly applaud. We can set our eyes to see God look at us as we enter Heaven saying, "Well done, good and faithful servant."

When Heaven is our home, we don't fear death. Death is only a moment, but our eternal life will go on forever. Heaven is real. It's glorious, and it's everything we could ever imagine it being and more. It's the best reward for this life because God is there!

MAIN THOUGHTS TODAY

- Heaven is our real home
- We belong to the Trinity
- We are passing through this earth
- While we are here, we are ambassadors

ADD FIVE MINUTES TO YOUR STUDY

1. FOOD FOR THOUGHT

"Do not let your hearts be troubled. You believe in God; believe also in me. My Father's house has many rooms; if that were not so, would I have told you that I am going there to prepare a place for you? And if I go and prepare a place for you, I will come back and take you to be with me that you also may be where I am." **JOHN 14:1-3 (NIV)**

Jesus has gone ahead of us and has prepared a place for you in Heaven. It will be ready and waiting when you arrive home. Your place there is assured and certain.

2. THINGS TO 'CHEW' ON

"So we are ambassadors for Christ.." **2 CORINTHIANS 5:20 (AMP)**

AMBASSADORS

Since we belong to Heaven, God considers you ambassadors for Him. The word "Ambassador" comes from the Greek word Presbuo. It describes an ambassador or one who fulfills the duties of an ambassador. It has a very similar meaning in scripture as it does in the dictionary. Here are a few main thoughts:

1. A diplomatic official of the highest rank, sent by one sovereign or state to another as its resident representative.

2. A diplomatic official of the highest rank sent by a government to represent it on a temporary mission, as for negotiating a treaty.

3. A diplomatic official serving as permanent head of a country's mission to the United Nations or some other international organization.

4. An authorized messenger or representative.

God wants your heavenly citizenship to help empower you to live as an authorized messenger. You have full authority! Let me tell you, when Heaven is backing you up, they are behind you. Their primary objective is to provide for you, help you, and assist you. Think about some ways in which you are an ambassador to your circle of influence.

BELONGING TO A FAMILY

—— DAY TEN ——

STORYLINE: JESUS LIVED WITH THE DISCIPLES AS FAMILY AND SERVED THEM. IN THAT WAY HE DEMONSTRATED THAT CHURCH IS NOT AN EVENT, BUT RELATIONSHIP. CHURCH IS THE FAMILY HE INVITES US TO BE A PART OF.

"Every church needs to grow warmer through fellowship, deeper through discipleship, stronger through worship, and larger through evangelism."
RICK WARREN

SPIRITUAL FAMILY

When each of the disciples sat at the table with Jesus during that final evening, he washed their feet and ate with them. He had become their family; they were brothers now. Their spiritual family had become stronger than their natural family. It was clear they had become close. Jesus was leaving the earth, but they had lived alongside Him; watching and learning how He did life. Gathering, eating, and remembering were all part of the lifestyle, part of the call. They were called to belong to the family of God now.

They followed a daily discipline of worship in the Temple followed by meals at home, every meal a celebration, exuberant and joyful, as they praised God. People, in general liked what they saw. Every day their number grew as God added those who were saved. Acts 2:46–47 (MSG)

Another version says, "And the Lord added to the church daily those who were being saved." The Aramaic word for "church" is the joining to "meet" and "come." It gives the picture of being invited, an invitation. God is always inviting us to join His family. The invitation is always in our hands, waiting to be opened.

The word "church" in the Greek is ekklesia which means "called-out ones." Each of us has been called out of the world and set apart. If we live in the fullness of our faith, we will live with a picture of heaven in our eyes, Christ in our hearts, and hope for His return in our souls.

Pull all these meanings together, and it gives us a clear picture of what God intended His ekklesia to be. We are the "called out ones," and we are invited to come and meet. Church isn't just a place we go and meet; it's a place to belong. Church isn't an event; it's relationship.

MEALS AT HOME

Also, don't you just love the tradition of the New Testament church? "They followed a daily discipline of worship in the Temple followed by meals at home, every meal a celebration, exuberant and joyful, as they praised God." They would head to church but afterward they would eat together.

Some of my favorite childhood memories are of the meals we shared with others after church. Both of my parents were hippies and gave their hearts to Christ in during the Jesus Movement. Back then no one had much money. They lived in communities, on properties, and ranches. They would gather for church every week, and once the service was over, they would pull out huge tables and cover them with cloths. Everyone would bring a dish to share. Yes, all my southern friends know this as a potluck. As a little girl, I remember spending almost the whole day with our church. Worshiping, eating, playing, running around and making memories. Some of those relationships we still have today. They became family.

Life isn't that easy for most of us, but I believe it's God's plan to put each of us in a family. How does He do this? By calling us to a church commu-nity. If we saw the church as a family and less like an event, we may be more faithful to go regularly.

"… you will know how people must conduct themselves in the household of God. This is the church of the living God, which is the pillar and foundation of the truth." **1 TIMOTHY 3:15 (NLT)**

Let me say a few things. I've given my life to the church, and before I could even walk, I was traveling to churches around the world. I've been in charismatic, conservative, missionary, pentecostal, community, de-nominational, almost anything you can imagine in 39 years of living this life. One thing is for sure; the church is flawed. It's true. Mainly because it's run by humans and last I checked it's impossible for a human to see everything as clearly, and in the same way, as another human. Leadership is a hard place to be. Secondly, no two churches are alike. Not even if our core values or fundamental doctrines align. We just come out different, like our kids.

Find a church. A place where you can belong. Look for other citizens of heaven that are living with eternity in mind. Serve them. Love them. Forgive them. You are called out to belong to them. They are your family! Sit at the meal of salvation together. Take the bread and wine together in remembrance. Eat the meal that will never run out. Eat food that satisfies even your deepest hunger. Live in joy, live in a community. It's God's greatest desire!

MAIN THOUGHTS TODAY
- Jesus invited the disciples into His inner circle; they lived as family.
- Jesus was among them as Savior, yet He washed their feet. We serve each other.
- So much of their fellowship involved food and sharing it!
- Church is not an event—it's relationship; we are the church.
- God invites us into His family; the church.

ADD FIVE MINUTES TO YOUR STUDY
1. FOOD FOR THOUGHT

"Jesus didn't respond directly, but said, "Who do you think my mother and brothers are?" He then stretched out his hand toward his disciples. "Look closely. These are my mother and brothers. Obedience is thicker than blood. The person who obeys my heavenly Father's will is my brother and sister and mother." **MATTHEW 12:48–50 (MSG)**

That phrase 'obedience is thicker than blood' accurately captures the essence of the church family. But how incredible is this piece of scripture after He had just been told that His actual mother and brothers were outside?! He used it to illustrate the strength of the bond we are meant to feel with one another as brothers and sisters in Christ.

"The bloodline of Jesus is thicker, deeper, stronger than the bloodline of race, ethnicity and family." **JOHN PIPER**

2. THINGS TO 'CHEW' ON

"I've loved you the way my Father has loved me. Make yourselves at home in my love. If you keep my commands, you'll remain intimately at home in my love. That's what I've done—kept my Father's commands and made myself at home in his love. "I've told you these things for a purpose: that my joy might be your joy, and your joy wholly mature. This is my command: Love one another the way I loved you. This is the very best way to love. Put your life on the line for your friends. You are my friends when you do the things I command you. *I'm no longer calling you servants because servants don't understand what their master is thinking and planning. No, I've named you friends because I've let you in on everything I've heard from the Father.* **JOHN 15:10–15 (MSG)**

We are linked through love and obedience; particularly the command to love one another. The verse that says, "Love one another the way I loved you" is extraordinarily challenging. Pause a moment and reflect on the way you love others; particularly other Christians—those you attend church alongside. Are you fulfilling this? The answer if we're not is that we need MORE of His love.

_____

_____

_____

_____

_____

"Don't be harsh or impatient with an older man. Talk to him as you would your own father, and to the younger men as your brothers. Reverently honor an older woman as you would your mother, and the younger women as sisters." **1 TIMOTHY 5:1–2 (MSG)**

While some of us may not have known our earthly father or mother, the instruction is clear here. We are to treat the church family with tenderness, respect, honor, and protection. We need the power of the Holy Spirit to be His ambassadors here on earth!

_____

_____

_____

_____

_____

"Suppose you see a brother or sister who has no food or clothing, and you say, "Good-bye and have a good day; stay warm and eat well"—but then you don't give that person any food or clothing. What good does that do?" **JAMES 2:15–16 (NLT)**

We are also to take care of those in the church family that are less fortunate than ourselves; providing for their needs when we have more and vice versa so that no one goes without.

MILK +HONEY

HUNGER TO BECOME

"Those who live in fear will not travel very far in their journey of self-actualization. "Fear is restrictive.. Those who step into their fears know the joy that comes with the learning, and the growth that comes with the courage to step into the unknown. Often what we fear the most is what our heart is calling us to become. It scares us because it matters that much."

SUSYN REEVE[5]

So we've looked at our hunger to be loved and our hunger to belong. We have seen that both of these hungers being met is critical to the wellbeing of our soul. And remember the journey from child to adult, and how society and upbringing can work against us as we try to find out who we truly are and where we belong? We are shaped by our desire to fit in. We don't want to miss out or be rejected so we become somebody other than our real or true self, as God designed us.

Abraham Maslow was a human psychologist born in 1908 in Brooklyn, New York. He is best known for his development of the theory now known as "Maslow's Hierarchy of Needs" as he began to understand what motivated people. He saw that some human needs were more powerful than others and so divided them into five general categories, from most urgent to most advanced: physiological, safety, belonging/love, esteem, and self-actualization.

We have loosely covered the first four, and our pilgrimage this week is the journey of becoming. Simply put, we look at unpacking what it looks like to become, and how we can go about it.

The discovery of self-actualization (in Maslow's Hierarchy) refers to the need for personal growth and discovery that is present in all of us. Maslow states that a person is always 'becoming' and never remains static[6]. Perhaps he knew his Bible! Perhaps he knew the ways of God and how He is always shaping us and changing us!

The point is, it is in our human nature (because we are made in the image of God) to be growing and changing throughout life. This week as we look at the journey the Israelites took to their Promised Land, we will see that they had an opportunity to grow and become more than they were at the point they arrived on the borders, but they chose not to. They remained

5. The Inspired Life: Unleashing Your Mind's Capacity for Joy
6. http://www.simplypsychology.org/maslow.html

'static' and were, therefore, doomed to stay as they were and wander for 40 years without inheriting the good, the wonderful and the better that God had in store for them.

The dictionary definition of self-actualization says, 'The realization or fulfilment of one's talents and potentialities' and gives an example sentence: 'The key to self-actualization, though, is that it specifically involves the striving towards the development of oneself as a unique individual.'[7] If we take that into the context of our life with God and our journey of becoming, again, it speaks of movement, of decision making for change. Yes, God is always working on our behalf and is changing us moment-by-moment, day-by-day and there are times when He is extremely close and seems to be taking care of all our needs without us asking. But as any good parent does, sometimes He steps back to see how we will manage and what we will decide when faced with a challenge or decision. Will we trust Him?

Think of it like teaching a toddler to walk. When they start off, the parent is holding both of the child's hands and leading him around. This helps strengthens the little guy's legs. Gradually, the parent attempts to let go; holding maybe just one hand, but eventually letting go all together. If you've ever done this with a child you can remember their eyes widening with horror the first time you let go! "NO, Mommy!" they're thinking. Why? Because they don't think they can do it. You've been 'doing it for them' for the last little while and they liked that. And when they try, and fall, they cry and give you a look of, 'I told you so!' Why do we let go? Because we know they can do it and we want to see the look of utter delight on their face when they realize they can! It's the joy of every parent to see a child become an adult.

Does it sound familiar? It's the same with God. Can't you just see the Israelites' journey through that same lens? God had been leading them on a journey and 'doing it for them.' He provided a rescuer who walked them right out of Egypt after a display of some incredible miracles. He split the sea right in front of their eyes so they could walk across it and He provided food for them every day. Then, as they arrived at the outskirts of the Promised Land, the moment came when He 'let go' and waited to see if they would step up to the plate and remember who He was and what He had done as they faced contending with the giants that were occupying their land.

7. https://en.oxforddictionaries.com/definition/self-actualization

They didn't...and do you know why? Fear and apathy. Some of them were afraid and some of them were lazy. They'd grown used to being parented and didn't want things to change. They were afraid of change and afraid of changing.

As we look at their journey this coming week, keep in mind that God is so for you becoming all that He has destined you to be. He has your fully 'self-actualized' self in His mind's eye and every challenge you face is an opportunity to partner with Him to become that person! So let's get started!

LEAVING TO BECOME
— DAY ELEVEN —

STORYLINE: YOU ARE LOVED, AND YOUR PRIMARY NEED IS TO BE LOVED. YOUR VALUE NEVER CHANGES, BUT YOUR EFFECTIVENESS DOES. ONCE YOU EAT AT THE TABLE OF VALUE, YOU BEGIN TO BECOME MORE EFFECTIVE.

"What we know matters but who we are matters more." **BRENÉ BROWN**

BELONGING TO BECOME

After we come to a place where we know we are loved and belong, we start to become. It's impossible to hang out with someone consistently without becoming like them. We are created to become what we behold.

The Greek word for 'becoming' is gínomai. It means to emerge, become, the transition from one point (realm, condition) to another. I love this meaning! When we start to become like Christ and become who He has called us to be, we have to transition. We go from one place to another. Our God identity begins to emerge.

Let me explain...

VALUE VS EFFECTIVENESS

Imagine if I walked down the street and found a penny. The penny looked brand new, like it had never been put to use, or touched. After walking a few more steps, I found another penny. This one looked beat up. It had been tossed around, handled and was worn down in appearance. Holding both of these pennies in my hand, side by side, you could see their appearance was very different. And if later that day I was in need of some change to pay for something, which penny could I use to pay? If you said either of them, of course, you would be correct. Why? Because they both have the same value. It doesn't matter how much the penny had been used, beat up, or how old it was, they both hold the same value.

To God, we each have the same value. It doesn't matter if you are as pure as when you entered the earth, or you've been around the block a few times. We will always hold the same value. God doesn't look at my four-year-old son Beckham any different than He sees me. On paper, I've done a lot of things for Christ. I've been an ordained minister for over a decade, written books, preached messages, prayed for thousands of people; I could go on and on. Beckham... well, he can barely wipe his butt. He hasn't written one book, preached one message, prayed for one person or given one dime to Christ. But he still holds the same value to God as I do.

Value is not based on what we do. Value is based on who we are. Beck and I hold the same title in Heaven: a child of God. Our value comes from this reality. Nothing else we do or don't do can change the way God sees us. We are His, He is ours, Jesus paid the same price for us, and that makes us valued.

So why then, do we do all the things we do? Why not lock ourselves up in some jungle hut on a tropical island to live in peace and wait to die, knowing we are all going to end up in the same place? It has everything to do with effectiveness, not value. We build, grow, cultivate and demonstrate for the sole purpose of being effective. It matters because God is trying to feed the earth a meal of salvation and we are the servers.

GOD'S PEOPLE

In the Old Testament God's people found themselves in a place where their value hadn't changed, but their effectiveness was at a standstill.

Moses had left his family, a royal Egyptian adoptive home and now lived far away from Egypt with his wife and son. He was hoping to lay low. Stay out of trouble. One day he's confronted with a burning bush. God got his attention through this engulfed shrubbery and started speaking to him. He now had Moses' full attention!

God said, "I've taken a good, long look at the affliction of my people in Egypt. I've heard their cries for deliverance from their slave masters; I know all about their pain. And now I have come down to help them, pry them loose from the grip of Egypt, get them out of that country and bring them to a good land with wide-open spaces, a land lush with milk and honey, the land of the Canaanite, the Hittite, the Amorite, the Perizzite, the Hivite, and the Jebusite.
EXODUS 3:7-8 (MSG)

God heard their cry. They were His people. His most valuable possession. They had been eating the food of slaves. Food that kept them bound. Food that kept them dependent. A meal that fed them just enough but never left them full.

God wants them to sit at a new table. A table with plenty of room. A good table. A buffet overflowing with milk and honey. A place of abundance. But they would have to come out to enter. The food of freedom doesn't come cheap or easy; there's a cost. You may have to get the taste of Egypt out of your mouth before you cross over into your promised land. But God is with you in the transition.

MAIN THOUGHTS TODAY
- When we are loved, and we belong, we start to become
- Our value stays the same, our effectiveness grows
- God has a promised land for you to transition into
- The journey won't be easy, but God is with you

ADD FIVE MINUTES TO YOUR STUDY
1. FOOD FOR THOUGHT

"My identity as a Christian has always had more to do with becoming than simply being. And what I have always wanted to become has been fully alive and deeply human." **DR DAVID G BENNER**

Your journey of becoming matters. It matters to God and it matters to the world because you are part of His plan and purpose. More than that, God wants you fully alive, enjoying abundant life and bang smack in the middle of your Promised Land doing what you were born to do. Let's run after Him for the same thing!

2. THINGS TO 'CHEW' ON

"If you're brave enough to leave behind everything familiar and comforting, which can be anything from your house to bitter, old resentments, and set out on a truth-seeking journey... and if you are prepared, most of all, to face and forgive some very difficult realities about yourself, then the truth will not be withheld from you." **LIZ GILBERT, EAT PRAY LOVE**

Our value will never ever change, but our effectiveness can. As I mentioned earlier, the journey is not easy. We will need to let go of some things and choose other things like trust, faith, love, forgiveness, etc. He doesn't do this to make it hard work. He wants you to succeed! Ponder for a few minutes and write down at least one thing you know you need to let go of.

The Israelites were uncomfortable with the journey; it was unfamiliar to them. It caused them to fear and then to grumble. Are there things God is asking of you or places He is asking you to go that are having a similar effect? Pause and write them down. Consider if these might be part of His journey to get you into the Promised Land.

_____

_____

_____

_____

_____

_____

_____

_____

_____

_____

_____

_____

_____

_____

_____

_____

_____

_____

_____

_____

_____

_____

_____

_____

_____

_____

_____

_____

ROOM TO EAT

— DAY TWELVE —

STORYLINE: GOD'S DESIRE IS TO BRING YOU INTO A SPACIOUS PLACE. HE WANTS TO GIVE YOU A PLACE TO BELONG AND A PLACE TO BECOME. OUR LIMITATIONS TO 'BECOMING' EXIST IN TWO PRIMARY PLACES: OUR ENEMY AND OURSELVES. YOU MAY BE FED THREE MEALS A DAY, BUT YOU MAY STILL BE A SLAVE. FREEDOM REQUIRES US TO LEAVE WHAT FEELS NORMAL, NEUTRAL AND SAFE. WE HAVE PERMISSION TO BE FREE!

"The spacious, free life is from God, it's also protected and safe. God-strengthened, we're delivered from evil— when we run to him, He saves us." **PSALM 37:39–40**

SPACIOUS LIVING

Many years ago I was at a place in my heart where I had stopped dreaming. I don't mean in my sleep, but for my life. I felt dull. I was bored. I was doing all the right things, but I wasn't alive on the inside. I'll never forget God speaking to me one day. He said, "Havilah, you need to take yourself more seriously. I take you very seriously." As He was talking, I knew I was being invited to live life differently, to see possibilities, not just limitations.

"...bring them to a good land with wide-open spaces, a land lush with milk and honey,..." **EXODUS 3:7–8 (MSG)**

After reading this verse, a part of it stayed with me. God had a desire to bring the Israelites out to a spacious place. He wanted to give them a place to belong but also a place to become. God didn't want them limited by anyone. He didn't want them enslaved by others. His desire was for them to be fully themselves. Fully free. Fully alive. Complete. He wanted them to become all He had designed them to be.

God's desire for His people now, two thousand years later, is the same. Paul's words written to the Corinthian church could have been spoken to the Israelite people during their captivity. At the same time, His words are relevant to us now and could be pulled forward and be spoken right into our lives.

Dear, dear Corinthians, I can't tell you how much I long for you to enter this wide-open, spacious life. We didn't fence you in. The smallness you feel comes from within you. Your lives aren't small, but you're living them in a small way. I'm speaking as plainly as I can and with great affection. Open up your lives. Live openly and expansively! **2 CORINTHIANS 6:11–13 (MSG)**

LIMITED LIVING

The limitations we often feel aren't always from God. Remember, you have a real enemy. He would love to keep you bound, limited, dependent, and weak. He may be feeding you just enough to satisfy your daily desires, but you're not living a full and satisfying life because his meals are scraps; a counterfeit. He would love to stop you moving forward and keep you from growing, emerging, becoming.

Your limitations can also be external physical limitations that you were born with or internal in the form of limiting self-beliefs because of your upbringing.

I grew up with learning difficulties. I had a hard time with reading, comprehension, and writing. I remember a time in my life where I felt humiliated at school. I walked through each class praying no one would ever see my papers, my grades or, God forbid, ask me a question in class. My whole upper-grade school years were about me hiding, lying to others about my success and hoping never to be exposed. When I gave my heart and life to Christ, I had to overcome very real personal limitations.

My greatest enemy wasn't the devil but myself and my fear. It was normal for me to eat at the table of hiddenness and feast on being limited; I didn't understand how God was going to bring me out into an open space. I couldn't imagine sitting at a table where there was plenty of room to grow, to be myself, to take all the time I needed to become.

By faith, Moses, when grown, refused the privileges of the Egyptian royal house. He chose a hard life with God's people rather than an opportunistic soft life of sin with the oppressors. He valued suffering in the Messiah's camp far greater than Egyptian wealth because he was looking ahead, anticipating the payoff. By an act of faith, he turned his heel on Egypt, indifferent to the king's blind rage. He had his eye on the One no eye can see, and kept right on going. By an act of faith, he kept the Passover Feast and sprinkled Passover blood on each house so that the destroyer of the firstborn wouldn't touch them. **HEBREWS 11:24–28 (MSG)**

FOOD OF SLAVES

It's interesting, but the Israelites ate very well while in captivity. Most of us would have thought that, as slaves, their food would have been reduced and limited. But if we study the story we find they had plenty of food to eat The Egyptians understood the slaves were their workforce. They needed them to be in peak physical condition.

Bondage doesn't always look like lack. It can be a place in our lives where we are reduced to one source. Only sitting at one table. Eating expensive food but it's the food of slaves. It leaves us living a dull, dreary existence. It may be easy to come by, but it's not your Promised Land. It's not your wide open space, flowing with milk and honey. When we find ourselves in a place where we have chosen to just BE rather than BECOME we are living in a dangerous place.

MAIN THOUGHTS TODAY
- God wants you in a spacious, free life
- He invites you to follow Him to transition out of slavery
- The two obstacles to moving are yourself and your enemy
- Bondage doesn't always taste bad. Beware staying still!

ADD FIVE MINUTES TO YOUR STUDY

1. FOOD FOR THOUGHT

"The history of a man's relationship with God is the story of how God calls him out, takes him on a journey, and gives him his true name. Most of us have thought it was the story of how God sits on his throne waiting to whack a man broadside when he steps out of line. Not so. He created Adam for adventure, battle, and beauty; He created us for a unique place in His story and He is committed to bringing us back to the original design... There comes a time when you have to leave all that is familiar and go on into the unknown with God." **JOHN ELDREDGE; WILD AT HEART**[8]

The journey of becoming is full of 'adventure, battle and beauty' as John puts it here. Yes, we have choices to make and fears to face but if our eyes are on what lies on the other side; if our eyes are on the Promised Land with all its abundance, milk and honey, then we are more likely to step out of our place of slavery and trust God to lead us safely through.

2. THINGS TO 'CHEW' ON

"The smallness you feel comes from within you. Your lives aren't small, but you're living them in a small way... Open up your lives. Live openly and expansively!"

8. ransomedheart.com/daily-reading/there-comes-time-when-you-have-leave-all-familiar

2 CORINTHIANS 6:11–13 (MSG)

Your beliefs about who you are affect your ability to get to the spacious place. Take a moment to ask the Holy Spirit to help you capture some of your self-talk. What are some of the limiting things you are saying about yourself? Write them down.

_____

_____

_____

God thinks way more highly of you and invites you to step out of those beliefs and see yourself the way He does. Ask Him how he sees you and write down what He says, even if you don't think (yet) that it could possibly be true.

"The thief approaches with malicious intent, looking to steal, slaughter..."
JOHN 10:10A (VOICE)

Our enemy wants to keep us small, fearful and hiding. He imprisons us by throwing lies at us, playing on our insecurities that we are not good enough, brave enough, etc. so that we end up feeling frozen to the spot, unable to move forward. How true is this for you right now? Ask the Holy Spirit to reveal where the enemy is keeping you immobilized and write it down.

_____

_____

_____

_____

God is calling you out into a spacious place; into the unknown where the only certainty is Him. Will you respond? Take a few moments to read the story of Peter stepping out of the boat in Matthew 14:26–36 and apply it to the above area where you feel immobilized. What would it take for you to move forward? Make notes.

_____

_____

_____

_____

Did Peter end up drowning? In the Message it says, "Jesus didn't hesitate. He reached down and grabbed his hand." As you step out and take risks, He will always, always catch you.

FLOWING
— DAY THIRTEEN —

STORYLINE: LIVING FROM A PLACE OF OVERFLOWING IS THE PLACE GOD DESIGNED FOR US TO LIVE. WE OFTEN FIND OURSELVES MALNOURISHED BECAUSE WE DON'T UNDERSTAND THE NEEDS OF OUR SOULS AND HOW TO FEED OURSELVES.

"...to bring them up from that land to a land [that is] good and spacious, to a land flowing with milk and honey [a land of plenty]..." **EXODUS 3:8 (AMP)**

LIFE OVERFLOWING

I've always imagined, as I read this verse, a sort of fantasy land. Where the waterfalls are of rich, creamy milk and the pools of water are of rich, thick honey. A kind of Willy Wonka Promised Land. Have you thought of that, too? Ha! As much as I wish there were such a place here on earth, the Biblical meaning is a little more practical.

"Fruit trees grow in many different terrains, but their produce overflow with nectar only when the land is especially fertile when the trees are particularly well-nourished."

"Similarly, livestock survives in many habitats, but they only overflow with milk when they are in particularly fertile pastures.

Thus, a "land flowing with milk and honey" is indicative and symptomatic of a greater good—the fertility of the Promised Land."[9]

The keyword is "flowing." It's not a one time, glad you came, high five! It's a consistent flow that originates from a place of peace, love, and belonging.

Now let's break this down practically.

---

9. chabad.org/library/article_cdo/aid/624194/jewish/Why-is-Israel-called-the-land-of-Milk-and-Honey.htm

PRACTICAL FREEDOM

When we choose to sit at the table of bread and wine, we will live an entirely different life. Our life is marked with confidence because we are deeply loved, and we know we belong. Our belief leads us to start hearing God's voice in our daily lives. As we do, the places of bondage or our limiting beliefs will be exposed. God's voice is always a narrative of freedom.

The way the Bible explains our Promised Land isn't as a particular place, but a way of life God promised us we could live.

JOHN 10:10 SAYS, *"The thief comes only to steal and kill and destroy. I came that they may have and enjoy life, and have it in abundance [to the full, till it overflows]."* [10]

He came to give us life, the kind that is full, flowing, and overflowing. Doesn't that sound familiar? God promises the Israelites a place of flowing abundance. A tangible reality of God's blessing on their lives. We are promised the same internal reality today.

I wish it were always this simple, but often we struggle with enjoying a life in the flow. It seems like we are stuck somewhere outside of Egypt, in the wilderness and nowhere near the Promised Land.

Let me explain some of the difficulty we all experience at some time in our spiritual lives.

UNDERSTANDING YOUR SOUL

Each of us is made up of three parts: spirit, soul and body. Our spirit comes alive the moment we invite the Holy Spirit to live inside of us.

But if God himself has taken up residence in your life, you can hardly be thinking more of yourself than of Him. Anyone, of course, who has not welcomed this invisible but clearly present God, the Spirit of Christ, won't know what we're talking about. But for you who welcome Him, in whom he dwells—even though you still experience all the limitations of sin—you yourself experience life on God's terms. It stands to reason, doesn't it, that if the alive-and-present God who raised Jesus from the dead moves into your life, he'll do the same thing in you that he did in Jesus, bringing you alive to himself? When God lives and breathes in you (and he does, as surely as he did in Jesus), you are delivered from that dead life. With his Spirit living in you, your body will be as alive as Christ's! **ROMANS 8:10-11 (MSG)**

God's Spirit works perfectly, and His primary objective is to lead you to live in relationship with Christ. Your body is called the temple of God. Simply put, our bodies host His presence: His Holy Spirit.

10. John 10:10 AMP

Our soul is our mind (where thoughts originate), our emotions (where our feelings arise), and our will (where our determination and decisions derive). Our soul isn't automatically renewed the moment we are born again. The Bible says we need to go to work and partner with the Holy Spirit to renew our minds, which then, in turn, influences our emotions and behaviour.

Our souls can keep us from living in our Promised Lands. Our carnal minds and desires, unsurrendered wills, and frantic emotions can keep us from experiencing an overflowing life. When we choose to align our thoughts with Christ and eat from His table, everything begins to flow and we become a place of abundance. Nothing may have changed on the outside, but on the inside transformation is taking place.

MAIN THOUGHTS TODAY
- Jesus' promise when He came was that we have an abundant, full life
- As we hear God's voice, places of bondage and limiting beliefs will be exposed
- Our spirit comes alive the minute we give our lives to Christ.
- Our soul can keep us from the Promised Land and leave us in the wilderness
- We need to partner with the Holy Spirit to be transformed so we can move forward

ADD FIVE MINUTES TO YOUR STUDY
1. FOOD FOR THOUGHT

"...I came that they may have and enjoy life, and have it in abundance [to the full, till it overflows]" **JOHN 10:10B**

Your spirit is transformed the moment you give your life to Christ. From that moment on you have the same resurrection power living in you that raised Him from the dead, together with the guidance from His Holy Spirit. You are set up for success to make it on this journey towards the abundant life!

2. THINGS TO 'CHEW' ON

"Our souls can keep us from living in our Promised Lands."
HAVILAH CUNNINGTON

Our soul is made up of our mind (thoughts), our emotions (feelings), and our will (determination and decisions). These three aspects of our soul have been 'running the show' before we got saved. Journal what this looked like for you.

_____

_____

_____

_____

_____

_____

_____

_____

_____

_____

"So, my brothers and sisters, you owe the flesh nothing! You do not need to live according to its ways, so abandon its oppressive regime. For if your life is just about satisfying the impulses of your sinful nature, then prepare to die. But if you have invited the Spirit to destroy these selfish desires, you will experience life." **ROMANS 8:12–13 (VOICE)**

The role of the Holy Spirit is to help us transition from a life led by our wilful desires and frantic emotions to a life led by the Spirit. Take a moment with each aspect and ask the Holy Spirit to highlight an area in your life that is still under the influence of a wilful desire or emotion that He is wanting to help you with so that you can experience abundant life. Journal.

_____

_____

_____

_____

_____

_____

MILK+HONEY
— DAY FOURTEEN —

STORYLINE: HUNGER IS THE ONLY THING THAT GETS US TO MOVE ON. GOD PROMISES US THAT WE CAN TASTE AND SEE THAT HE IS GOOD. WE HAVE TO WANT TO SIT AT HIS TABLE AND EAT. HIS WORDS ARE OUR FOOD. HIS WORDS HOLD PROMISES THAT KEEP US FULL.

"Each of us has a promised land for our lives. God's promises are key to us entering into the vision that God has given us. If you are in a desert God is ready to take you out! Time to move on from eating manna to eating the food that God freely gives in the promised land of your destiny!"[11] **JOHN BELT**

THE TASTE OF FREEDOM

I'm one of those people who eats at the same place over and over again; inevitably, I wear it out. I'm not the first one in my family to start this tradition. I come from a long line of jilted joint goers. It happens slowly. At first, I discover a place. I fall head over heels. My week is then consumed with me coming up with lame excuses to pop into my favorite place and try the dish one more time. It gets even worse. I find ways of weaving my new addiction into most of my conversations hoping to convert one more person. As most fires die out, mine slowly fades. The thought of eating that meal transfers from a 'Can I?' to a subtle 'Should I?' and eventually an 'I don't want to.'

The taste of freedom, for the Israelites, was the sweetest thing they could have imagined eating. The Promised Land of milk and honey was almost more than they could imagine. Let's be honest, moving over one million people from slavery to freedom was no small feat. They needed to get hungry. Their hunger for a different life had to become the thing that propelled them to seek a new land.

Why did God use the words milk and honey?

---

11. http://www.elijahlist.com/words/display_word.html?ID=9631

Milk symbolizes superior quality, the richness of taste, and nourishment. Honey represents sweetness. The goodness of the Promised Land, Canaan, is both nourishing and pleasant.

The words of God's promise about this new land painted such a vivid picture: a table spread out as long as the Israelite nation. Teeming with milk, fruit, honey, fish, cucumbers, watermelons, leeks, onions, garlic, anything to their delight.

GOD'S PROMISES

The same is true for us when God speaks. He gives us a promise. He paints a vivid picture for us of His table where all are welcome to dine. Eating a meal of deep abiding love, feasting on indescribable joy, devouring bread and wine—the meal of salvation. It's available anytime we come respond to His invitation.

Most people think they are hungry for this meal, but find that they are not. They continually eat f at the wrong tables. Leaving full, embarrassed, ashamed but quickly dissatisfied with the 'fast food' the enemy offers. Only a desperation to be free will take you to a place where you are willing to leave those other tables and only eat in your Promised Land. That desperation will take you from one meal to a land flowing with Milk and Honey.

Where do we find this table in our modern lives? How do we feast on meals that satisfy the soul?

God created us with bodies and souls. Both require sustenance for life. What food is to the body, hope is to the soul. When our body needs energy, we eat food. But when our soul needs hope, how do we "eat" God's words? We eat God's promises![12]

It is written, "Man shall not live by bread alone, but by every word that comes from the mouth of God" **(DEUTERONOMY 8:3, MATTHEW 4:4).**

When a young Jewish boy first begins to study the Torah (first five books of the Hebrew scriptures), they take a drop of honey and put it on the page. They then have him lick the honey off the page, representing the sweetness of the Torah. Milk and honey are a type of food and studying the Word of God is food for the soul.

God's words, found in our Bibles, are His promises to each of us. A promise is a pledge of a good or better future for us. God's promises are what He pledges to be for us, do for us, and provide for us.[13]

12. http://www.desiringgod.org/articles/you-are-what-you-eat

13. http://www.desiringgod.org/articles/you-are-what-you-eat

God has used promises to feed saints throughout the ages.

For I know the plans I have for you, declares the Lord, plans for welfare and not for evil, to give you a future and a hope **JEREMIAH 29:11**

God also fed His people throughout their journey to the Promised Land. So you can be sure He will provide the nourishment of His promises to you as you journey to your promised land.

"Then the Lord said to Moses, "I will rain down bread from heaven for you. The people are to go out each day and gather enough for that day... At twilight you will eat meat, and in the morning you will be filled with bread... The Israelites ate the manna for forty years until they arrived at the land where they would settle down"[14]

Most of the time, when I find myself spiritually famished, it's because I'm eating at the wrong table and living a spiritually dull life. I'm wandering in the wilderness instead of hoping in the promises of God. My soul needs to be reminded of what's on offer: what He can do for me, be for me, and provide for me. Connecting to Him is my source of soul food.

MAIN THOUGHTS TODAY
- Hunger for something better is what moves us forward
- The promised land of God's table is both nourishing and pleasant
- God's Word and the promises contained in it feed us
- We must respond to His invitation and eat His promises if we want to be satisfied
- He will provide the food for your journey of transition

ADD FIVE MINUTES TO YOUR STUDY
1. FOOD FOR THOUGHT

"Our appetites dictate the direction of our lives — whether it be the cravings of our stomachs, the passionate desire for possessions or power, or the longings of our spirits for God. But for the Christian, the hunger for anything besides God can be an arch-enemy. Do you have that hunger for Him? If not, it is not because you have drunk deeply and are satisfied. It is because you have nibbled so long at the table of the world. Your soul is stuffed with small things, and there is no room for the great." **JOHN PIPER, A HUNGER FOR GOD**

This is a powerful quote. As you were reading today's study, you might have been thinking, "I used to be hungry for God; I wonder where that's gone." Is it possible that you have been 'eating' other things and that is what has crowded out your desire for God?

14. Exodus 16:4,12+35 (NIV & MSG)

2. THINGS TO 'CHEW' ON

"Then Jesus asked them, "When I sent you without purse, bag or sandals, did you lack anything?" "Nothing," they answered." **LUKE 22:35 (NIV)**

We've already seen how God provided for the Israelites for their entire journey from Egypt to the Promised Land. Here in Luke, Jesus is reminding the disciples of a previous journey He sent them on and asking them if they went without. They remember and say no. Not remembering God's provision caused the Israelites to slip into grumbling. He will provide for the Journey. Reflect on your history with God and remember times He has provided for you. Journal your response.

_____

_____

_____

_____

_____

_____

_____

_____

_____

_____

_____

_____

"Jesus said, "I am the Bread of Life. The person who aligns with me hungers no more and thirsts no more, ever." **JOHN 6:35 (MSG)**

These are the words of Jesus. This is a promise that we can feed on. It's the Truth; that if we respond to Him through obedience, trust, faith and love, we will lose the cravings in our souls for other things. Where do you think you are out of alignment? Journal and then ask God for a relevant scripture to help you come into agreement with what He says.

_____

_____

_____

_____

MILK+MEAT

— DAY FIFTEEN —

STORYLINE: OUR HUNGER FOR THE PROMISED LAND MOVES US FROM A PLACE OF BONDAGE TO A PLACE OF FREEDOM. THE PROMISE OF MILK AND HONEY IS ENOUGH TO GET US MOVING, BUT THE PROGRESSION OF MILK TO MEAT IS RE-QUIRED TO "TAKE THE LAND."

"Sometimes we have to face our fears, embrace the adventure, and take the plunge. But what holds us back from risking it all? How do we keep our eyes focused on the goal when everything is trying to distract us? Peter helps us answer those questions as he jumps—not off a cliff, but out of a boat. If we look closely enough we may just discover the courage to follow his example."[15]
DR. J.D. DAVIS, PASTOR

The Israelites were so close to the Promised Land they could almost taste the creamy 'milk' in their stomachs and the sticky sweet 'honey' on their lips. They ventured into the desert and up close and camped outside. When they went to scope out their Promised Land, they found it inhab-ited. People were living in their area and, worse still, they were giants! Seriously, God!? I can't even comprehend what that must have been like for them to find this out. "Wait... let me get this straight. We took God at His word. Pulling everything we owned, gathering our families, crossing the Red Sea. We ate manna every day for 40 years and now... now we are here, and there are giants in our land?!" Why would God have the Prom-ised Land inhabited? Why would they now need to fight for their land even though God promised it to them?

God didn't just want to give His people a Promised Land. He wanted to make them His people of promise. People who would dream about His goodness, deeply trust Him and believe Him; believe that He wouldn't bring them this far only to have them go back again or, worse, have them die in this dry and weary land.

15. http://www.lifeway.com/Article/sermon-leave-the-boat-peter-faith-matthew-14

Were the Israelites a people who trusted God? In the beginning, yes. But as their food faded so did their confidence. They started to complain and grumble. It got so bad in the camp, they ended up wandering for 40 years in the desert on a trip that should have only taken them 14 days and led them straight into their Promised Land. Their grumbling kept them in the desert. The only requirement for them to inhabit their Land was that they grew up. They were going to have to learn to eat a different meal. A meal of maturity. A meal of faith.

There's a time when every parent who has a healthy and growing child in their home has to transition the food their baby is eating. In the formative months, the baby drinks breast milk or formula. Milk is the safest thing for the baby to eat. His little body doesn't have the teeth to chew meat. It's straightforward and palatable. Eventually, the child begins to grow, and you start to introduce new foods. Milk becomes cereal, cereal becomes veggies and fruit and, eventually, their little vegan diet gets other adult foods added to it. It's a standard and natural progression.

Just like the natural, our spiritual life requires the same graduation.

I have a lot more to say about this, but it is hard to get it across to you since you've picked up this bad habit of not listening. By this time you ought to be teachers yourselves, yet here I find you need someone to sit down with you and go over the basics on God again, starting from square one—baby's milk, when you should have been on solid food long ago! Milk is for beginners, inexperienced in God's ways; solid food is for the mature, who have some practice in telling right from wrong. **HEBREWS 5:11–14 (MSG)**

Once the generation of grumbling Israelites had died out, God told Joshua that they were now ready and were going to have to "Take the Land." God laid out the plan to Joshua, down to who should lead the people and how many times they should march around Jericho, the first city He planned they would take. God was meticulous in His requests, and gave Joshua instructions which he then passed on to the people. He explains the game plan, and then says, "No one is going to talk as we march." God didn't ask them to be quiet...Joshua did! Why did he make this request? Think about it. If grumbling had kept them in the desert, grumbling would keep them out of their Promised Land. Joshua didn't want to take any chance of any more delays to their destiny. He wanted to be extra safe.

We quickly learned the people listened to Joshua, right down to the plea for silence. The thought of this many people listening and following through proves their developed maturity.

The promise of milk and honey pushed them into the desert, but the meal of meat was needed for them to take their land. The journey of becoming in our lives is less about a moment, and more about a lifetime of willingness to sit at the table of maturity. Progressing from the Milk of promise to the Meat of maturity is the only way to prepare us to eat the next meal of our lives; the meal to Bless.

MAIN THOUGHTS TODAY
- You have a destiny; a Promised Land to enter
- The Israelites' grumbling delayed entry into theirs
- Your attitude about where you are right now matters
- Maturity is the key to entering

ADD FIVE MINUTES TO YOUR STUDY
1. FOOD FOR THOUGHT

"If you have ever wondered why you have faced so many tests; so many giants who are like Goliaths in your life, it's because God is making a warrior out of you. He is preparing you for new and expanded places of authority and influence." **BARBARA YODER; TAKING ON GOLIATH**

We've looked at the Israelites' arrival at the Promised Land. They perhaps thought they would just walk in, so were shocked to find it was occupied by giants. What was God up to?! Remember, they had been slaves, so had grown used to a life of being spoon-fed. They were led through the desert and instead of growing up, they behaved like sulky teenagers and grumbled. God knew they needed some challenges to face; some obstacles to overcome in order to build muscle and become strong and mature, so here it was.

2. THINGS TO 'CHEW' ON

"We can't attack those people; they're way stronger than we are." They spread scary rumors among the People of Israel... *"Everybody we saw was huge... Alongside them we felt like grasshoppers. And they looked down on us as if we were grasshoppers."* **NUMBERS 13:31–33 (MSG)**

Your attitude to where you are right now in your circumstances matters. God knows exactly where you are and what you are facing. Do they feel insurmountable? Do any of them leave you feeling feel like a grasshopper? How are you responding? Do they leave you with fear, grumbling or apathy? Or maybe all of the above. Take some time to process this and journal.

"The Lord replied, "I have forgiven them as you asked. Nevertheless, as surely as I live... not one of the men who saw my glory and the miraculous signs I performed in the desert... will ever see the land I promised their forefathers." **NUMBERS 14:20–23 (NIV)**

After Moses and Aaron heard the reports, they waited on God and He spoke this to them. First of all, remember we are under the New Covenant; His mercies are new every morning and we have many, many chances because of grace. BUT, we also now know that our souls (those attitudes we've just looked at) can continually rob us of our Promised Land if we let them. The key to entry here is REMEMBERING what God has already done so that we are encouraged for the journey ahead. Take a moment and write down what you know of all of God's faithfulness and provision to you so far.

_____

_____

_____

_____

"For Caleb, though, it's a different matter. He's distinct from the others by having a different spirit[16] and has followed My lead wholeheartedly. I will make sure that he is able to enter the land and to live in it—he and his descendants after him." **NUMBERS 14:24 (VOICE)**

This was also part of what God spoke to Moses and Aaron. Wow, imagine that. So many of the Israelites missed out on the Promised Land; wandering for the rest of their lives in the desert and dying out there. Not Caleb. The key here is faith. God LOVES faith and cannot help but respond to it. Review your circumstances again through they eyes of faith. If need be, repent of how you are viewing them and responding to them. Journal your renewed response of faith.

_____

_____

_____

_____

"Joshua blessed him. He gave Hebron to Caleb son of Jephunneh as an inheritance... because he gave himself totally to God." **JOSHUA 14:13–14**

The book of Joshua is about the new generation of Israelites entering the Promised Land. In this chapter Caleb presents his case to Joshua of how he reported back differently and now he gets his inheritance, the Promised Land. God is faithful! All He looks for is that you remember who He is and what He has done and then respond to Him as He calls you forward from where you are into maturity and into YOUR Promised Land.

15. Caleb interrupted, called for silence before Moses and said, "Let's go up and take the land—now. We can do it." Numbers 13:30 (MSG)

FISH+
LOAVES

HUNGER TO BLESS

"The abundant life begins from within and then moves outward to other individuals. If there is richness and righteousness in us, then we can make a difference in the lives of others, just as key individuals have influenced the lives of each of us for good and made us richer than we otherwise would have been."

SPENCER W. KIMBALL

I love the story of Peter. He was actually called Simon when Jesus first met him. He was a fisherman, casting nets into the sea, catching fish and minding his own business. Along comes Jesus one day and spots him in a boat with his father and brother preparing their nets. They've been fishing all day and are tired and fed up because they haven't caught anything. Jesus gets in the boat with them and tells them to cast their nets once more. Simon Peter says, "..because you say so, I will let down the nets." When they did they caught so many fish the nets were in danger of breaking. Simon Peter falls to his knees. "Don't be afraid; from now on you will catch men,"[17] says Jesus. So Simon Peter leaves everything to follow Him.

All of a sudden his life is turned upside down and he finds himself living a very different kind of life; on the road instead of the sea. Living alongside Jesus, a man...the son of God; one who walks in the miraculous and is full of love, humour and wisdom. We are privy to Simon Peter's journey of becoming. Is it a smooth ride? No, of course not; it isn't for any of us. We watch him. He is passionate and impetuous and it gets him into trouble when he slices the ear off the centurion in the garden when the soldiers came after Jesus. But his rashness had boldness mixed in and he was the only disciple who had the courage to step out of the boat onto the water when he knew it was Jesus.

He's full of questions and yet at the same time he is the first one to answer when Jesus asks the disciples, "What about you, who do you say I am?" He says, "You are the Christ, the Son of the living God." Jesus recognizes the revelation that Simon Peter has had from heaven and prophesies over him that he will be foundational to the New Testament church and changes his name to Peter (which means rock), "And I tell you that you are Peter and on this rock I will build my church."[18]

17. Luke 5:10 (NIV)
18. Matthew 16:18 (NIV)

Buried deep inside of Peter's heart and spirit was a desire, a yearning, to make a difference. He desperately wanted to be like Jesus. You can feel his hunger as he is around Him. Asking questions, jumping to Jesus' defense when He is attacked. He is rebuked by Jesus on more than one occasion and still he keeps going. Until the moment when what Jesus tells him at the Last Supper comes true. He denies Jesus three times. He was utterly devastated and wept bitterly;[19] utterly horrified by his behaviour.

Jesus again appears to the disciples after his resurrection while they are fishing and calls to them to let their nets down on the other side. John says, "It's Jesus!" and as soon as Simon Peter heard him say, "It is the Lord,'" he wrapped his outer garment around him and jumped into the water."[20] Jesus tells them to bring some of the fish to the shore and says, "Come and have breakfast." While they are eating, he asks Peter three times, "Do you love me?" and Simon Peter answers "Yes." "Feed my sheep," is Jesus' response. The next time we see Peter he is standing up in front of crowds and in front of rulers, elders, and teachers of the law full of the Holy Spirit declaring the truth of who Jesus was. Unafraid, unashamed and full of the power of His love.

Do you see Peter's journey of becoming?! It was a bumpy ride. But he bounced back from failure, denial, impetuousness, rashness and foolishness. He took the rebukes of Jesus and let them shape him and mold him to become more like the Savior that he loved and adored. And he was restored over a meal.

Peter went from being your average fisherman into becoming one of the key founders and keepers of the New Testament church. How? He put what he had (his life) into Jesus' hands and followed hard after him. When we get to the book of Acts Peter is hungry to feed the church; hungry for the masses to experience the extent and depth of the love that Jesus had for them; hungry for them to understand the sacrifice that Jesus made in order that they could be reconciled back to the Father.

This is our final week and I'm so excited to think that by the end of this study you will look back on the journey that God has and continues to take you on—from a place of separation and shame to a place of overflow and passion. A place where you are so full, you can't help but be compelled to give out of the overflow.

19. Luke 22:62
20. John 21:7

LACKING TO BLESS

— DAY SIXTEEN —

STORYLINE: AFTER WE BECOME, WE HAVE A DEEP HUNGER TO BLESS. WHEN WE HANG OUT WITH A MIRACLE WORKING GOD, WE START TO SEE THOSE WHO NEED A MIRACLE AND WE FIND WE HAVE A DEEP HUNGER TO REACH OTHERS.

"The abundant life begins from within and then moves outward to other individuals. If there is richness and righteousness in us, then we can make a difference in the lives of others, just as key individuals have influenced the lives of each of us for good and made us richer than we otherwise would have been." **SPENCER W. KIMBALL**

HUNGER TO BLESS

Everyone wants to be great. You want to be great. Specifically, when you begin to hang around Jesus, you start to see life differently. What seems impossible is now possible. Blind eyes can see, deaf ears can hear, and those who couldn't walk are now running. Signs and wonders follow Jesus everywhere He goes because He is a miracle working God!

The disciples are doing life with Jesus. They have watched him do miraculous things. Their faith is growing in the reality that Jesus can change not just their nation but each life. The news of what Jesus was doing was spreading around the different villages, and thousands of people came out to meet Him. We land right in the middle of this scene; Jesus was slipping away on a boat to grieve the death of his cousin, John the Baptist, but He sees the crowd and has compassion on them.

When evening came, the disciples came to Him and said, "This is an isolated place and the hour is already late; send the crowds away so that they may go into the villages and buy food for themselves." But Jesus said to them, "They do not need to go away; you give them something to eat!" **MATTHEW 14:17–21 (AMP)**

Jesus is ministering and the day is slipping away. The disciples have a moment of compassion as well. They're looking at all of these families and thinking about their practical needs: to have a place to sleep and eat.

Sometimes in our attempt to serve Jesus, we are so focused on the situation in front of us, we fail to look up and see Him and the big picture. We can end up serving the principle rather than the person of the Prince of Peace and what He wants to do. Often we begin to explain to Jesus about the needs of the people because we think that maybe He's missing something... or maybe He's too busy to notice. We don't always understand what's happening, and if we can't see the bigger picture, we get busy planning. The danger is our compassion can be a distraction to the miracle God wants to perform.

Jesus looks at the disciples and puts the challenge back in their court. "You give them something to eat!" Can you imagine Jesus looking at these disciples and telling them to give them something to eat?

It's important to remember that there were five thousand men counted, but that did not include the women and children. This is a Biblical way of counting crowds. When we read there were five thousand men, we can easily double and triple that number to account for the women and children. The total of people sitting in that crowd, listening to Jesus, is around 15,000 people! Can you imagine looking around and seeing 15,000 people that need to eat? And it's not just that they are going to go hungry but they also have nowhere to sleep.

When Jesus says to them, "You give them something to eat!" He was not so much saying 'meet their practical needs' —rather, He was inviting them to a new place of faith; to take part in one of the greatest miracles of all time. I have learned in my life that Jesus will often tell me to do things that seem completely out of my control or my capacity.

As a teenager, I remember going to my youth pastor about our worship team. At the age of 17 I believed I was an expert on all things life and, specifically, music. I explained to him that we (speaking on behalf of a group of us) were not happy with the worship and felt more could be done. If you imagine me as a strong, willful and sometimes brash 17-year-old, you would be right! I shared my heart, and he quietly listened. I explained that we had a small worship team that we had formed and could help their worship team. (I'm cringing even as I write this.) He looked at me and said, "Well, I think you guys should lead worship next week." I walked out of that room completely shell-shocked. It wasn't anything I thought was going to happen. He was the leader. He needed to fix it. The end. Walking with my tail between my legs, I pulled the band together. We did lead that night and every night for the next two years.

Years later, I became a Worship Pastor and served my church for eight years and I can trace it all the way back to that moment in his office. When the Pastor looked at me and said, "You give them something to eat!" I had a choice. I could either explain that, despite sharing my ideas for change, I wasn't ready, didn't have anything to give, or what I had wasn't enough, or I could go home, grab what I did have and bring it to Jesus.

MAIN THOUGHTS TODAY
- We all want to be great, especially when we're around a miracle working God
- We can get too focused on the practicalities of a task in front of us, when God instead wants to perform a miracle
- Jesus' invitation leads us into a place of greater faith; to be part of a miracle

ADD FIVE MINUTES TO YOUR STUDY
1. FOOD FOR THOUGHT

"If we wish to truly experience a life that makes an eternal difference, the power within us is not enough. It is the power God offers that matters.[21]"
DILLON BURROUGHS

You have a desire to be great and you were born to do great things. But your good deeds alone won't be enough without His power being allowed to be expressed through you.

2. THINGS TO 'CHEW' ON

"Meanwhile, the disciples were urging Jesus, "Rabbi, eat something."

But Jesus replied, "I have a kind of food you know nothing about."

"Did someone bring him food while we were gone?" the disciples asked each other. Then Jesus explained: "My nourishment comes from doing the will of God, who sent me, and from finishing his work." **JOHN 4:31–34 (NLT)**

Here is an example where the disciples have their mind set on what they can see with their human eyes and what they are hearing with their human ears instead of seeing the big picture. Jesus was always trying to get them to see things from heaven's perspective and to live by a different set of guidelines. Jesus' focus had been to interact with the woman at the well and bring her life; that was his food. Take a moment and ask God

21. Hunger No More: A 1-Year Devotional Journey Through the Psalms

to open your eyes today, as you encounter each person and situation, to see from His perspective. Come back and journal at the end of the day.

_____

_____

_____

_____

_____

_____

"One day Jesus said to his disciples, "Let us go over to the other side of the lake." So they got into a boat and set out. As they sailed, he fell asleep. A squall came down on the lake, so that the boat was being swamped, and they were in great danger. The disciples went and woke him, saying, "Master, Master, we're going to drown!" He got up and rebuked the wind and the raging waters; the storm subsided, and all was calm. "Where is your faith?" he asked his disciples." **LUKE 8:22–25**

So we looked at being in situations where we are so preoccupied with the practicalities of solving what's in front of us that we can miss that God wants to do a miracle. What about when storms hit and circumstances feel unstable? What do we do then? You'd think by now that the disciples would trust that if Jesus said, "Let us go over to the other side" that would mean they would get there. Jesus' response on being woken is, "Where is your faith?" Think for a moment about your life. Are there storms hitting you? Circumstances you can't control? Is it a moment to be flailing in fear or is it an opportunity to increase your faith?

_____

_____

_____

_____

_____

_____

"Be who God meant you to be and you will set the world on fire."
CATHERINE OF SIENA

God wants you to be great. He wants you to do great things. Once you have become, you can go bless the world and set it on fire!

MAKING THE LUNCH

—— DAY SEVENTEEN ——

STORYLINE: IN YOUR ORDINARY EVERYDAY LIFE YOU ALWAYS HAVE INGREDIENTS FOR A MIRACLE. YOU JUST NEED TO LOOK TO HIM AND SEE WHO AROUND YOU NEEDS THE MIRACLE THAT HE CAN WORK THROUGH YOU.

"Having a vested interest in other souls unconditionally creates a ripple effect that produces miracles in the lives of those around us." [22]
MOLLY FRIEDENFELD

They replied, "We have nothing here except five loaves and two fish."

Before I had children, I would take care of other people's kids. Whenever I had a big task to do that might get a little messy, I always found a way to preoccupy the kids. My job was to keep the house clean, safe, and orderly for Mom and Dad's return. After having my sons, my approach completely changed. I found myself always looking for ways to involve my littles. The mess, order, and even the risk aren't as important as their ability to learn, grow, participate and eventually grow in skills. Skills they will take with them for life.

Jesus wasn't a babysitter. He wasn't on a mission to keep the kids (aka the disciples) clean, safe and in order until their Father could return. No! Jesus was a Father. He desperately wanted the men to get involved and jump into the realities of heaven. He was very clear that His mission on earth was to demonstrate risk. The risk he took in raising men up, as sons, would eventually make them Men of God.

When Jesus told the disciples to feed the people, He wasn't mocking them. Clearly feeding 15,000 people would have been an insurmountable task. He was making a statement. I believe He was trying to show them everything from a different angle. Can we feed the people as Jesus asked? No. What next? Let's look around and see what we have.

22. The Book of Simple Human Truths

Look and see is precisely what the disciples did. They had already looked around the crowd asking if anyone had food to share, eventually finding a boy who offered his two fish and five loaves of bread to the team. It was all they had. They took it to Jesus.

It's easy to go right to the two fish and five loaves, but I've often asked the questions while reading this part, "Who packed this lunch? Was there a Mom at home? Was she just doing what she does every day?" There are so many moments in the Bible where we find ordinary people doing ordinary things, and it becomes an extraordinary moment. Was this Mom just doing regular life and yet it turned out she was preparing the elements of one of the greatest miracles Jesus ever performed?

We can often assume the opportunity to bless comes at a spiritual moment—the moments when we feel most "spiritually available." I can't find that in the Bible. I only see God performing miracles at mystery moments. I have tremendous hope when I think about it. God will use moments in our lives, when we're doing ordinary things and can't imagine God doing anything with it, to bless a whole lot of people.

I remember a young mom in our church. She and her husband loved God, faithfully served our community, and were a part of our faith family. Each of them always found ways to love people well. Even though they were going through a very hard season financially, they were always giving. His job kept getting pay cuts, and they began to live off help from the government. At the time, there was a gentleman in the church running a supply company. He had over-ordered for a particular job and there were leftover boxes of diapers, paper towels, cereal, cleaning supplies; you name it. He heard about this family in need, so he drove over to their home in the middle of the night and put all the leftover items in a big pile in their front yard. When the family woke up, they ran out to see their front yard full of all kinds of supplies. The mom told me she just cried and cried. To him, it was merely leftover supplies, but to the family, it was a miracle.

After God asks us what's in our hands, we have two options. We can become discouraged by our personal lack; focusing on our meager income, insufficient time, absent gifts and abilities, and vacant opportunities. Or we can pull ourselves together, and start looking at what we do have and bring it to Him. If we don't judge where it comes from or how much it is, we may be holding the very ingredients of a miracle waiting to happen.

There was a woman in the Bible whose dead husband's creditors were threatening to take her two boys as payment for his debts. She cries out to Elisha the prophet for help and he says, "How can I help you?" and asks her what she has in the house. She explains that she doesn't have "anything at all, except a little oil." The prophet tells her to bring it to him. As he pours the oil, the miracle happens. It begins to flow and flow and there was no stopping it. In fact, it continued to flow until the widow tells him she has run out of jars. Then he says, "Go, sell the oil and pay your debts."[23]

Today, I want to you ask yourself what meal you can make for someone in your life? Do you think you have nothing? Do your two fish and five loaves embarrass you? Don't let them. God loves to prepare meals through our lives, to bless the world.

We'll talk about that more tomorrow ...

MAIN THOUGHTS TODAY
- In the ordinary everyday life, Jesus is looking to perform a miracle
- Look at what you have as the ingredients for a miracle
- Bring it to Jesus
- Look around and see who needs a miracle

ADD FIVE MINUTES TO YOUR STUDY
1. FOOD FOR THOUGHT

"While Jesus was still speaking, someone came from the house of Jairus, the synagogue leader. "Your daughter is dead," he said. "Don't bother the teacher anymore." Hearing this, Jesus said to Jairus, "Don't be afraid; just believe, and she will be healed." **LUKE 8:49–50**

Wow—what a response from Jesus! How many of us would have said, "Oh, I'm so sorry. I got waylaid on the way and so many people wanted my attention. Let me help you with the funeral arrangements or pay for the burial." God wanted to perform a miracle and Jesus knew it so, without hesitation, He speaks. He then follows Jairus to his house and raises the little girl from the dead.

2. THINGS TO 'CHEW' ON

"To see your prayers answered, enter God's presence with thanksgiving and worship. Then rest in your secret place and meditate on His Scripture and words to you. Ask the Lord this question: "What is it that You want to do in these circumstances?" Then listen and wait until He answers and directs you how to pray."[24] **GRAHAM COOKE**

23. 2 Kings 4:1-7
24. Crafted Prayer

How did Jesus know what God wanted to do in the moment? How could He be so sure? Because He had spent time with the Father and learned what His voice sounded like so that when the moments came He could respond. To get good at something, we need to practice. Graham's experience here is helpful. Think of a circumstance and then give it a go.

_____

_____

_____

_____

_____

_____

_____

_____

_____

_____

_____

Once you've practiced the above for a little while, take it out into your daily life (where you don't have the time to wait on God for as long as you do behind closed doors) and ask Him to highlight people to you that need a miracle. See if you can hear what He wants to do. Journal your stories.

_____

_____

_____

_____

_____

_____

_____

_____

_____

_____

_____

_____

_____

BLESSED TO BLESSING

— DAY EIGHTEEN —

STORYLINE: YOU MIGHT NOT THINK YOU HAVE MUCH, BUT IF YOU BRING WHAT YOU HAVE TO JESUS, HE WILL BLESS AND MULTIPLY IT.

"In a world where very few people care if you live or die, there is a light that shines in the distance. It has a name that they call Hope and it carries with it people that never stop caring. They learned long ago that extending mercy was not a choice, but a place where God lives." **SHANNON L. ALDER**

He said, "Bring them here to Me." Matthew 14:18 (NIV)
God can't bless what you don't bring to Him.

Giving my life to Christ at 17 years of age was exhilarating. I wanted to do everything for Him! I remember telling Him, "God, I'll go anywhere you want to send me, I'll say anything you want me to say. I'm all in!" It was true. I had taken the leap; I was head over heels in love with my Savior. In my youthful zeal I convinced myself I wouldn't struggle with anything because, after all, I was serving God. It should be easy from here on out. Did any of you have the same expectation?

It wasn't until my first ministry trip that had a "come to Jesus" moment. I quickly began to realize that the struggles I had before I gave my life to Christ (learning, reading, writing, comprehension) were the same struggles I had after I gave my life to Him. I had thought God would take it all away and heal me.

One night I told God, "God, my hands are so empty. I have nothing to give you." Tears streamed down my face. I felt helpless. Humbled. He answered back. "I know Havilah, but one day your hands will be overflowing with the things I give back to you." I didn't know how He was going to do it; I just hoped He would. Now looking back at my life, it has become a reality. God did exactly what He said He would do. He has blessed my life to overflowing.

When the disciples came to Jesus with the fish and loaves, nothing had changed. The fish weren't magical fish that could quickly reproduce and the bread wasn't regenerating yeast. Nope. It was regular bread and your average fish.

I can only imagine the disciples bringing the food to Jesus. I'm not sure if they found themselves embarrassed with what they had. Did they have a hard time looking Jesus in the eyes as they explained the meager meal they had collected?

Or maybe they were upset and irritable, telling Jesus they had only come up with this food. In frustration they might have thrown their hands out showing Him this ridiculous meal; lacking any faith that He could save the day.

Regardless of any of that, they brought it to Jesus.

Jesus took the bread, and he blessed it. Can't you just see it? 15,000 people were watching Jesus take this meal and pray over it. I can barely hold it together as I write this in anticipation. Remember, they didn't even know Jesus could do anything at this moment.

"Bring them here to me," he said. And he directed the people to sit down on the grass. Taking the five loaves and the two fish and looking up to heaven, he gave thanks and broke the loaves. Then he gave them to the disciples, and the disciples gave them to the people. **MATTHEW 14:18-19 (NIV)**

Jesus took the meal that was brought to Him. He blessed it. Then He broke it up and handed it to the disciples to distribute. There is so much gold in these few words.

In our desire to bless the world, we must bring what we have to Jesus. Often it won't look like much. We may be embarrassed bringing it to Him. The thought of offering Him our gifts seems humorous and almost trite. We can't imagine Him doing anything powerful with the little we provide.

Are you embarrassed by what you are offering to Jesus?

Could it be that He knows exactly what you are offering?

Take a good look, friends, at who you were when you got called into this life. I don't see many of "the brightest and the best" among you, not many influential, not many from high-society families. Isn't it obvious that God deliberately chose men and women that the culture overlooks and exploits and abuses; chose these "nobodies" to expose the hollow pretensions of the "somebodies"? That makes it quite clear that none of you can get by with blowing your own horn before God. Everything that we have—right thinking and right living, a clean slate and a fresh start—comes from God by way of Jesus Christ. That's why we have the saying, *"If you're going to blow a horn, blow a trumpet for God."* **1 CORINTHIANS 1:27-31 (MSG)**

It's not those who have it together or come with full hands that Jesus uses. It's those that are willing to bring what they have to Him. Those that believe His blessing on their lives is all they need.

MAIN THOUGHTS TODAY
- The fish and loaves weren't humanly enough
- The disciples brought them to Jesus anyway
- Jesus blessed what they brought and multiplied it
- He can do more than you ask or imagine with what you bring

ADD FIVE MINUTES TO YOUR STUDY
1. FOOD FOR THOUGHT

"Saturday night after the service, we went to the kitchen to watch the cooks as they were frying the chicken. It took them all night to prepare for the Sunday lunch, as our expected total was for almost 1200 people. Because Heidi had gone out to the garbage dump and compelled the people to come in, the crowd had virtually doubled by noon. When the main chef saw the multitudes arriving, he ordered the cooks to begin to fry some small fish in order to feed everyone. The Lord had a different plan. To the chef's amazement, He began multiplying the chicken until every one of the hungry guests had their plateful, 2300 people in all! Hallelujah! Wow God, You are so awesome!

We've all read in the Bible how Jesus fed the multitudes then, but it's different and so much more fun to see Him do the same type of miracle today while allowing us to take a small part."[25] **GEORGIAN & WINNIE BANOV**

God is the same God today, yesterday and forever. Miracles of multiplication are still happening on the earth today in places where people are bringing their 'little' and asking God to multiply it for those around them who need a miracle. What a joy to partner with Him!

2. THINGS TO 'CHEW' ON

"We need to be like the crowd in the gospel story—we need to let Jesus satisfy us. Instead, we try being satisfied by everything else, and while everything that

25. http://www.openheaven.com/reports/details.asp?id=1968

God created is good, it is not God. If we let God satisfy us, then everything else is gravy—wonderful when we have it, but quite alright if we don't. Like the crowd in the gospel: we can share, we can be satisfied with little, we can allow God to multiply what we have." **BROTHER ABRAHAM**

On our journey of becoming and beginning to bless others, our eyes of hunger need to remain focused on the only One who can satisfy us. As this quote says, we need to let Jesus satisfy us. Are there other things that are satisfying you? Are you hungry for more of Him and hungry to be a miracle to someone else today through what you already have? Journal your response.

_____

_____

_____

_____

_____

_____

_____

_____

_____

"God can do anything, you know—far more than you could ever imagine or guess or request in your wildest dreams! He does it not by pushing us around but by working within us, his Spirit deeply and gently within us."
EPHESIANS 3:20 (MSG)

It's an incredible thing that the God of the Universe has set His resurrection power within us in the person of the Holy Spirit. It's even more incredible that He wants to work through us and expects us to do more than Jesus did! Spend some time thinking on this and perhaps craft a prayer to the Holy Spirit about His work in you. What is He up to right now in your life that is leading you to your wildest dreams?

_____

_____

_____

_____

_____

_____

_____

DISTRIBUTING THE BLESSING

— DAY NINETEEN —

STORYLINE: EVERY SPIRITUAL GIFT IS VALID AND NECESSARY IN ORDER FOR MIRACLES TO HAPPEN.

So God has appointed and placed in the church [for His own use]: first apostles [chosen by Christ], second prophets [those who foretell the future, those who speak a new message from God to the people], third teachers, then those who work miracles, then those with the gifts of healings, the helpers, the administrators, and speakers in various kinds of [unknown] tongues. **1 CORINTHIANS 12:28 (AMP)**

THE GIFT OF ORGANIZATION
I was at a staff meeting when I first came across the gift of organization. A brilliant young man was working for our church. He had laid down his Yale graduating status to take a low paid job on our staff. His job? Organize this crazy, dream chasing crew. He was always busy balancing the budget, crossing every 'T' and dotting every 'I.' He was meticulous, diligent and gifted.

At one point, someone in his or her enthusiasm shouted out over the meeting to him, "You are so good at keeping everything we are doing together!" He looked at them, smiling slightly, and said, "Well, you do know the gift of Administration is in the Bible." I thought he was joking. I went home that day, quickly jumping on my bed and pulling out my Bible to look for this hidden truth. He was right. Right in the middle of all those "spiritual gifts," administration was standing tall.

In our desire to bless, we can often forget that God is not just a God of crazy and wild miracles, but He's also the God of the balanced books, orderly gatherings, structured growth, and strategic advancement. If it weren't important to Him, He wouldn't have put administration as one of His spiritual gifts.

Looking back to our story yesterday, you can quickly see why order is important to Jesus.

They answered, "We have only five loaves of bread and two fish—unless we go and buy food for all this crowd." (About five thousand men were there.) But he said to his disciples, "Have them sit down in groups of about fifty each." The disciples did so, and everyone sat down. **LUKE 9:13-15**

Do you see it? The part where Jesus instructs the disciples to put everyone in groups of 50. I'm sorry... what? 15,000 people in groups of 50? How long must that have taken? It's interesting that Jesus wanted to perform a miracle, but He also needed the place to be organized. Could it be that organization prepares us for a miracle?

I remember the time God told me to stay out of debt and live within my means. I was a young woman and I didn't have large bills or a family to take care of, but I always lived by this request. I never bought things I couldn't afford. I didn't go on vacations in hopes the money would come in. I purposed in my heart to drive the car I could afford, buy a house with a down payment and never use credit to build a life. Was it easy? Not at all. I cut coupons, planted gardens, ate at home, discount shopped and through it all I was able to keep my commitment to the Lord. Now, looking back, it was the best thing I could have done for my future. My diligence to organize my life and stay on track has been catalytic in my ability to contain the miracles God has worked in my life.

The Greek word for the spiritual gift of administration is 'Kubernesis.' This is a unique term that refers to a shipmaster or captain. The literal meaning is "to steer" or "to rule or govern." It speaks of someone who guides and directs a group of people toward a goal or destination.

With this gift the Holy Spirit enables certain Christians to organize, direct, and implement plans to lead others in the various ministries of the Church. This gift is closely related to the gift of Leadership, but is more goal or task oriented and is also more concerned with details and organization.

Are you good at organizing? Do you thrive in structured environments? Good. God wants to take your gift of administration to help set the structure to contain and distribute His miracle working power. Never allow the enemy to belittle or devalue the gift you have to offer and the part you have to play. The church needs your contribution just as much as they need pastors, prophets, and teachers.

MAIN THOUGHTS TODAY
- Organization, or Administration, is a spiritual gift
- Jesus asked the disciples to organize the crowd so they could receive the miracle
- If we take responsibility to steward what we have, God sets miracles in our lives
- All gifts are necessary to contribute to the miracle

ADD FIVE MINUTES TO YOUR STUDY
1. FOOD FOR THOUGHT

"Moses had the gift of administration. In one night he organized over a million people to do the same thing, the same way, at the same time—that's administration. He led the same people from slavery to freedom out of Egypt, through the Red Sea, to Sinai—that's administration. He received plans for the building of the Tabernacle by revelation and coordinated its construction including all the internal and external details. Moses must have been able to think in such a way as to retain the exact instructions for this project—that's administration." **PAUL MANWARING**

We have, according to Paul in this same blog post, vastly misunderstood the gift of administration; thinking of it as merely clerical or office work. It is actually a powerful gift. Could it be that you are underestimating the gift or gifts that God has given you?

2. THINGS TO 'CHEW' ON

"Another biblical word linked to administration is oikonomia [oikos = house or home, nomos = the law; the "law of the home"]. It occurs seven times in the New Testament and means 'management, administration, plan, stewardship and putting into effect', in essence steering a household or family towards a desired outcome or vision."[26] **PAUL MANWARING**

We all have a responsibility to steward what God has given us. Look at the parable of the talents. If we want more we must use what we have and do what we can. Today. And then again tomorrow. Spend a few moments thinking about the fact that the Trinity are all phenomenal Administrators. They have and are steering you towards a vision towards things you cannot even imagine. Ask them today what your assignment is. How can you be their eyes, ears and hands for the person in front of you?

26. http://www.paulmanwaring.com/posts/the-importance-of-administration
27. http://www.paulmanwaring.com/posts/personal-discovery-series-part-1-p-is-for-passion

_____

_____

_____

_____

_____

_____

_____

_____

_____

_____

_____

_____

_____

Rediscovering God's original plan for each of us begins with passion, with the simple question, "What do I love?" But the reality is that it is not the simplest of questions, often far from it—and yet it may be the most powerful question we can ever ask or be asked. Knowing what we love will unlock your passion, not just for you, but for others, for the degree to which we know what we love will affect how much we love ourselves and therefore how much we can love our neighbors as ourselves."[27] **PAUL MANWARING**

Our journey into this study started by looking at our need for love and belonging. We are well on our way towards becoming, but love is never forgotten. Passion must be kept alive and love must be stewarded and cultivated in the secret place. It's a lifetime's journey. How is your passion? And can you answer the question Paul asks, 'What do you love?" Take some time to journal.

_____

_____

_____

_____

_____

_____

_____

_____

_____

_____

OVERFLOWING
— DAY TWENTY —

STORYLINE: WE GET TO GIVE TO OTHERS AND BLESS THEM OUT OF THE OVERFLOW THAT WE HAVE RECEIVED.

"and they all ate and were satisfied. They picked up twelve full baskets of the leftover broken pieces." **MATTHEW 14:20 (AMP)**

DESIRE TO BLESS
The moment we give Jesus our lives, He is ready to perform the miracle in us and through us that He's been waiting to perform.

Our desire to bless isn't something we came up with on our own. The heart to reach our world is in the DNA of every believer. It's not something we have to try and receive in some prayer line...and hoping Jesus gives us a heart to reach the world. Nope. It's not something we have to find or implant in us because it's already dwelling within us.

The Holy Spirit is now living inside of us. His primary purpose is to help us, comfort us and care for us, but also to reveal to us what the Father is doing and saying over our lives. What do you think the Father's primary objective is for the earth?

I'll cut to the chase. His greatest desire, and His burning passion, is that ALL WOULD BE SAVED. That all would come into the full knowledge of God. What do you think He is wanting the Holy Spirit to awaken in us on a daily basis? A desire to reach the world by revealing the miracle working power of Jesus Christ in the earth.

EVERYDAY PEOPLE
When the disciples brought the food to Jesus, He could have easily distributed the miracle by way of another miracle. After all, He wasn't hindered by human realities. He could have placed the food in everyone's hands in a moment. Bada boom, bada bing! I believe Jesus restrained Himself to demonstrate a greater message. The main purpose of the

'feeding of the 5000' wasn't the feeding. The more significant message was to demonstrate that He wants to partner with and work through everyday people, like you and me, to distribute the miracle.

VITAL ROLE

Why does God love the church so much? Because he designed the church to be a place where miracles can be contained, cultivated, and distributed. He wants each of us to play a vital role.

Your desire to bless and make a difference is exactly as God intended it to be. If your life is only about watching other people live and distribute the miracle, is it any wonder you are bored out of your mind? No wonder life seems mundane and routine.

What if every day you woke up ready to distribute the miracle? What if, instead of waiting for someone else to do the work of the Kingdom of God, you woke up believing that God was inviting you to take part in a miracle and you took personal responsibility to help? I think our world would change.

God has given each of us ingredients to make a meal. It may not be a meal that feeds 15,000 people, but I'm confident, if you trust Him, you can feed someone.

I'll never forget the day when God and I had a conversation about my table. He asked me, "Who is sitting at your table?" I saw huge tables with the thousands of people I have the honor of reaching each year with the message of Jesus. God said, "No, not that one... look for the other one." Then I saw a picture of my home and our little kitchen table. I saw my family sitting around it. The Lord said, "That is your most influential table. It's the most important meal to me." I knew He was right. I began to see my life in a way I had never seen it. I had a congregation of four, our young sons who needed discipleship. They needed the miracle of heaven distributed to them on a daily basis, and I was the one God called to do it.

The Bible says, "They picked up twelve full baskets of the leftover broken pieces." **MATTHEW 14:20 (AMP)**

Why would they have leftovers? Wouldn't Jesus know how much to give? Jesus wanted to provide them with a picture of how heaven works. When we bring our little to Jesus He can multiple it until you can't contain the overflow of the miracle. God doesn't just give us one seed in each fruit to plant. He gives us multiple seeds in every piece of fruit.

Your life is a fruitful life. If you take what you have and bring it to your table each day you won't have to turn people away. You will just have more to give because that's the Kingdom and that's the nature of our miracle working God.

I love the saying, "When you have more than you need, build a longer table, not a higher fence."

MAIN THOUGHTS TODAY
- Our desire to bless others is a spirit given part of our nature
- The main message of the fish and loaves is that He wants to include you!
- We are ordinary people called to do extraordinary things
- When God performs a miracle, we get to enjoy the overflow

ADD FIVE MINUTES TO YOUR STUDY
1. FOOD FOR THOUGHT

"...if anything matters, then everything matters. Because you are important, everything you do is important. Every time you forgive, the universe changes; every time you reach out and touch a heart or a life, the world changes; with every kindness and service, seen or unseen, My purposes are accomplished and nothing will be the same again." **WILLIAM PAUL YOUNG, THE SHACK**

You are important. What you carry is important. Your wiring and gifting is important. It will make a difference to the many, many people that cross your path. Do not underestimate or despise the small acts that you carry out every day that represent Him. You are making a difference and as you keep putting what you have into His hands, He will multiply it into a harvest!

2. THINGS TO 'CHEW' ON

"Once you have found the joy of being in God's presence and being overwhelmed by His love, you are enabled to share His miraculous power with everyone you meet. God is longing to release His miracle working power through you."[28] **KATHERINE RUONALA**

We get to be the blessing and a miracle to those all around us; in our families, our communities, our workplace. One of the keys to believing we can be a blessing is to be so full of God and His love that we are compelled to love. Set a goal this week to spend extra time in His presence. Ask Him to overwhelm you with His love.

"The only way to consistently do Kingdom works is to view reality from God's perspective. That's what the Bible means when it talks about renewing our minds. The battle is in the mind. The mind is the essential tool in bringing Kingdom reality to the problems and crises people face. God has made it to be the gatekeeper of the supernatural."[29] **BILL JOHNSON**

Another key to seeing and being a part of miracles in our own and other's lives is to believe. The Bible says that believing comes by hearing the Word of God and we must allow the Holy Spirit to take the words of God and change the way we think so that faith can rise. Perhaps spend some time looking at all the other miracles that Jesus did. What gets in the way of you believing you can do what Jesus did and greater?

"A woman noticed something intangible, something without definition. Her sickness drove her to the desperate act of touching a man in public, though she was "unclean." In desperation, she touched His clothing and became well.[30]

Jesus never taught about this secret to the miraculous, either before or after her miracle. Obeying a command did not heal her. She simply noticed the ways of the Holy Spirit upon Jesus and cooperated. The grace environment that surrounded Jesus invited people to explore. She was healed when she responded to an opportunity that no one else could see. However, once she experienced her miracle, her story spread.

By the time we get to the end of Mark 6, everyone who touched Him was made well. Even then, He never taught on the subject. He just lived as an open invitation for all to seek the One who desired to be found.

This adds an interesting insight to the possible effect of every believer who desires to live as Jesus did. The Holy Spirit upon us is accessible by others."

As we journey to become, let Him be the reason, so that we can pour out on others out of the overflow on our lives. The world is hungry for Him and He is waiting to feed them through us!

28. Mindset for Miracles series

29. The Supernatural Power of a Transformed Mind Expanded Edition: Access to a Life of Miracles

30. Matthew 9:20

31. http://www.charismanews.com/opinion/33485-bill-johnson-naturally-supernatural

STUDIES / DEVOTIONALS

EAT PRAY HUSTLE

Eat Pray Hustle is a 20 day Bible study derived from the life of Abraham. He was a man just like us, and he was on the road to his promise. He had a dream deposited in him as a seed, and he was doing everything he could to help it grow. He was eating, praying, and hustling most days... just like many of us!

This whole study is designed to help you understand the attributes of a God Dream. We will uncover what a Dream Chaser looks like and the signs of your greatest dreams revealed. We will expose what Dream Killers look like and what we can do to stay protected. We will learn to nurture the dream, care for it and live it out. Understanding these truths will change your life and give you a lasting legacy of fulfilled promise."

I DO HARD THINGS

"I Do Hard Things is a 20-day devotional study that will equip and teach you how to climb out of places of pain in your life. Whether you're a new or seasoned believer, thriving or maintaining, or just hungry for growth, this study will teach you how to persevere through the process so you can walk in confidence and lack nothing (James 1). Most people were not taught how to persevere through trials and, therefore, spend their days avoiding pain or ignoring it. It's time to stop and learn how to do hard things. Havilah's casual, inclusive, and light-hearted style will give you vision for the journey and tools to use along the way. Isn't it time to learn how to do hard things?"

RADICAL GROWTH

"The pathway to the radical growth you're wanting is not complex. It's not some unattainable, envy-provoking vision or dream meant to torment you with its impossibility. However—let's be honest, no one has a vibrant life by accident. No one has a flourishing garden unintentionally.

Simply put, VIBRANT LIVING LOOKS LIKE A LIFE GROWN ON PURPOSE.

With clear understanding of God's heart toward you, a commitment to 100% obedience, and an unrelenting determination to follow truth, radical growth is possible. It's a life that's within your reach! This practical guidebook will give you daily access to begin your own journey of living a radical and vibrant life!"

THE GOOD STUFF

"The Good Stuff study is a 20-day guidebook to finishing strong! Many of us are great at starting things, but not so fantastic at finishing them. In Hebrews 12, it says we are to strip down, start running and never quit! So, how do we do this? How do we run our race in such a way that honors God, and leaves us successfully crossing the finish line?

I invite you to explore what God's Word has to say about four key areas in our lives: our mind, our will, our words, and our enemy. When we are fully engaged in these areas, we can't help but finish well. No matter your age or history in God, I encourage you to get the good stuff of the Word on your training belt—in your vocabulary, your bones, and in your spiritual muscles—so you can be renewed and empowered to finish your race strong!"

TRUTH ᵀᴼ TABLE

Our mission is to reach as many people as possible with the truth of God's Word through video based products, practical resources, and lifestyle tools.

Our vision is to inspire you to practical, wholehearted devotion to Christ. We've created many video based learning tools and books to help you follow along. We hope you start wherever you find yourself today and grow a vibrant relationship with God.

We want to invite you to grab a virtual seat at our kitchen table. Wherever you find yourself in life, we believe the next steps are worth taking. Truth to Table is all about discovering who God created you to be and how to move forward into your amazing destiny.

GET ACCESS TO A FULL LIBRARY OF VIDEOS INCLUDING BIBLE STUDIES, COURSES, VIDEO SERIES ON LEADERSHIP, PRACTICAL LIFE LESSONS AND MORE...TRUTHTOTABLE.COM

ENHANCE YOUR BIBLE STUDY
Video Bible studies and teachings that give you a starting point for your daily devotions.

FITS INTO YOUR SCHEDULE
Quick and easy lessons for the modern lifestyle. Anytime. Anywhere. Any device.

INTERACTIVE GLOBAL COMMUNITY
You don't have to go it alone. Connect with other truth-seekers through our platform.

STAY CONNECTED

website *havilahcunnington.com*

facebook *Havilah Cunnington*

twitter *@mrshavilah*

instagram *havilahcunnington*

youtube *youtube.com/user/havilahcunnington*

email *info@havilahcunnington.com*

FOR MORE INFORMATION
email info@havilahcunnington.com

join our newsletter

REQUEST HAVILAH TO SPEAK

WOMEN + STUDENTS + CHURCHES

FOR
*Retreats, conferences, one-night gatherings,
church services, leadership events*